HOW TO IDENTIFY PLANTS

Also by H. D. Harrington
Manual of the Plants of Colorado

HOW
TO IDENTIFY
PLANTS

by

H. D. HARRINGTON
Professor of Botany and Curator of the Herbarium
Colorado State University

Illustrated by L. W. Durrell
Emeritus Professor of Botany
Colorado State University

SAGE BOOKS, Denver

PREFACE

The purpose of this book is to provide practical help for those interested in learning the special technique of identifying plants. It is based on the writer's experience in watching several thousand beginners acquire this skill. Unfortunately there is no easy way, no "royal road" to this knowledge. Like everything else worth while in life it takes effort and perseverance. An attempt is made here to smooth out some of the rough places on the road but the real job must be done by the student himself.

The procedure followed in dealing with the necessary technical terms is to present the common ones in a special chapter where related concepts can be compared with each other. It is suggested that these terms be memorized by the student. The more unusual ones can be looked up as needed in the illustrated glossary that makes up the final chapter. The definitions of many of these terms have been deliberately simplified in order to give a practical instead of a theoretical treatment. The real test in drawing up these definitions was how the term was used in the average manual for the identification of plants. The illustrations are intended to present the general concept and therefore are not drawn from actual specimens. A picture is a static thing but the concept it represents may be a variable one. Sometimes a series of drawings is used to represent this range of variation - when only one is given it shows an average. The specimen will rarely if ever look exactly like the drawing but must conform to the general concept of the descriptive term as illustrated by it.

TABLE OF CONTENTS

Chapter I

INTRODUCTION

WHY WE NEED TO IDENTIFY PLANTS.

Many people are interested in learning the names of the plants growing about them. The motives behind this desire are probably many but it may be of interest to list some of the commonest ones as expressed to the writer.

1. To satisfy a general curiosity.

Usually the first question that comes to mind when one is confronted with a new and strange object is, "Now what is the name of that?"

2. To be able to talk or write about the plant.

When an object must be designated again and again then some sort of name for it becomes a real need. As one person expressed it to the writer, "Why, even a wrong name is better than no name at all!" It might be possible to talk about plants or keep written records concerning them, if each was designated by an arbitrary number, but the procedure would certainly be both tedious and unsatisfying.

3. To be able to look up information about the plant.

The great storehouse of human knowledge contains recorded facts concerning many species of plants. Questions may arise like the following. Is the plant edible? Is it poisonous to man or to his livestock? How palatable is it to animals? Does it have a tendency to become a weed and if so how can it be controlled? How should it be treated in cultivation? Does it have any special legend or interesting story connected with it?

These questions and many others may be answered very completely in various publications. However, all this information is ordinarily unavailable to the student if the name of the plant is unknown. If the first question is "What is the name of that?" then

1

the second often is, "What good is it; what is it used for?" Knowing the name of a plant opens the door to the answer to such a question.

HOW NAMES OF PLANTS CAN BE LEARNED.

The names of plants can be learned in at least two ways.

1. Ask someone who knows.

This method is satisfactory when dealing with rather few numbers and when your authority is constantly at hand. Probably this is the most enjoyable way of learning the names of plants, as a boy who becomes acquainted with trees by having them pointed out by his father. However, few of us have this opportunity of constant expert advice. Add to this the fact that our trusted authority may turn out to be a broken reed and we may learn a lot of incorrect names! It is just as hard to learn the wrong names as the right ones. The sad fact seems to be that the less some people know about plants the surer they are in making snap identifications! A real expert is always cautious, sometimes exasperatingly so!

2. Learn to identify the plants yourself.

This is the best and surest way because you can determine plants anywhere and at any time. All that is necessary is the correct manual or flora and the skill to use it. As indicated in the preface this skill is not easy to acquire. The writer periodically receives a desperate request, "Please tell me an easy method of learning to identify plants." There just isn't any such thing. Popular treatments and picture books of plants may be satisfactory if all that is wanted is a superficial viewpoint but they can never lead to a real fundamental knowledge of the subject.

WHY PLANT IDENTIFICATION CANNOT BE MADE EASY.

1. There is a special knack involved.

Some people pick up this skill more quickly than others. Discouragement always comes at the beginning when progress seems slow.

2. Technical descriptive terms must be mastered.

These terms are freely used by the manuals because they have a definite and exact meaning that cannot be expressed in ordinary language, at least with reasonable brevity. For example, two related species may differ only in the type of hairs on the leaf surface, one "tomentose", the other "pilose". This is a clear cut difference to one who understands these terms but almost impossible to state briefly in anything but botanical parlance. At least three ways of mastering these technical terms are possible.

(1.) Deal with each new term as it is encountered. Almost every manual includes a glossary explaining these terms.

(2.) Attempt to memorize all or most of the terms used by the manual and try to understand their exact meaning before starting the identification proper.

(3.) Drill on the important terms that are continually used and look up the others as needed.

The writer believes that the third method is the best for students. The first one slows the work down so much that a beginner becomes discouraged. The second method would surely work out but it would certainly be monotonous and uninteresting. The last procedure allows one to understand these commonly used terms better by giving a chance to compare related ones. For example the exact meaning of "lanceolate" as a leaf shape (Fig. 107) becomes apparent when one compares it with the related "linear" (Fig. 106) and "ovate" (Fig. 108). This third plan is the one on which this booklet is based. The next eight chapters are given over to a discussion of the terms that have been found to be most important. It is suggested that the student becomes so familiar with them that they need not be looked up each time they are used. An illustrated glossary is presented as the last chapter to aid in the understanding of the less commonly used terms.

Some students find it worth while to keep a list of each new term with its definition. These can be reviewed from time to time. However, some of the

3

names on this list may be uncommon and may not be used again for some time. Form the habit of checking the meaning of each new term as it comes up. Trying to get the meaning from the context, comparing it with its contrasting term, skipping over the phrase and trusting to luck - all these methods may work in certain cases but can never lead to a real skill in identifying plants.

3. Constant practice is necessary.

This means that a student must be really in earnest about acquiring the skill. Either a stern necessity or an unflagging determination (or both) are prerequisites in learning to identify plants.

The most efficient method of acquiring this technique is to learn it under the direction of some competent teacher where help can be given when it is most needed. However, many people in various walks of life have picked up this discipline entirely on their own without the aid of a formal course in the subject. Some of them have even become world wide authorities on special plant groups or on the flora of a limited area. A few have even wound up as teachers of the subject. Remember, do not allow yourself to become discouraged at first. Acquiring a skill or any special knowledge is much like rolling up a snowball - it appears to grow so slowly at first but enlarges with satisfying rapidity when it begins to attain a large diameter.

NECESSARY EQUIPMENT.

1. The manual or flora covering the area.

These will be discussed in a later chapter.

2. Hand lens.

A good lens is a necessity, probably something between an 8 X (8 times magnification) and a 12 X. The lower powered ones are larger and give a bigger field with a longer working distance. The higher powered ones are smaller and therefore easier to carry but although the image is magnified more it is not so clear. A good lens has a reasonably long working distance and gives a reasonably clear image even out toward the edge of the field. A common type of hand lens is shown in Fig. 1 A.

4

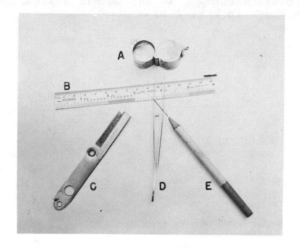

Fig. 1.

3. Forceps and needles.

These implements allow for the handling of minute parts. The forceps are shown in Fig. 1 D., a needle in Fig. 1 E.

4. Razor blade.

A sharp blade is needed in order to make thin sections of flower ovaries. An ordinary knife blade is not satisfactory even when very sharp. A straight edge razor works nicely if kept keen-edged. Most students prefer to purchase a package of one-edge safety razor blades, discarding the dull ones from time to time. A holder for razor blades is on the market and may prove to be a convenience. Such a razor knife is shown in Fig. 1 C.

The blade should be used with a pulling or pushing diagonal motion, not a chopping action but more on the order of manipulating a saw than an axe. This is illustrated in Fig. 39 in Chapter IV.

5. Rule.

Be sure the rule is graduated in centimeters and millimeters; practically all manuals and floras give

measurements according to the metric system. Such a
rule is shown in Fig. 1 B.

Chapter II

HOW PLANTS ARE CLASSIFIED

Before the technique of identifying plants is
developed the student should have in mind the way
plants are grouped together and how these various
groups are organized. It is often amazing for a beginner to observe how strikingly plants can be seg-
regated into various divisions and subdivisions. For
example, species of the genus Rosa the world over
have an unmistakable stamp of the "rose" upon them.
Man has attempted to recognize and name these natural
groupings. It is true that intergradations do exist
in some groups with exasperating regularity. We are
apt to notice these exceptions as we would one ob-
streperous child among a group of well behaved ones
and forget the fact that the great majority of plants
actually seem to group themselves naturally into
large and small units.

NEED FOR CLASSIFYING.

Several hundred thousand species of plants exist
in the world. A recent estimate placed the number at
335,000. The single state of Arizona was listed by
Kearney and Peebles in their Arizona Flora as having
132 families, 907 genera and 3,370 species. So even
the flora of one state poses a definite problem in
organization; somehow we must get the plants pigeon-
holed. In a herbarium it is necessary to file the
specimens away according to some system. We could
file them away in some artificial arrangement - as
for example trees, shrubs and herbaceous plants - or
we could arrange them alphabetically by name. Botanists have chosen to try to organize, classify and
group plants according to what they think has been
their evolutionary development, that is, in a phy-
logenetic system with related plants contiguous and
unrelated plants far apart.

A TYPICAL SYSTEM.

Species - the plants of one kind.
Genus - a group of related species.
Family - a group of related genera.

7

Order - a group of related families.
Class - a group of related orders.
Subdivision - a group of related classes.
Division - a group of related subdivisions.

The four divisions of the plant kingdom as outlined in many manuals and books on general botany
are:

1. Thallophyta (Thallophytes). The algae and
   fungi.
2. Bryophyta (Bryophytes). The mosses and
   liverworts.
3. Pteridophyta (Pteridophytes). The ferns and
   fern allies.
4. Spermatophyta (Spermatophytes). The seed
   plants.

The four groups are sometimes called phyla instead of divisions and some authors may not organize
them into categories of equal rank. You will want to
become familiar with the way your manual outlines
these major groups. Most ordinary books for the i-
dentification of plants include only the last two,
the so-called vascular plants. Of course special
manuals and treatments are available for the determination of species in the Thallophyta and Bryophyta
divisions.

CLASSIFICATION OF THE CINNAMON ROSE.

Let us see how the cinnamon rose would fit into
our scheme of classification.

Division - Spermatophyta - the seed plants as
    opposed to the other three divisions.

Subdivision - Angiospermae - plants with seeds
    borne in a closed ovary as opposed to the
    Gymnospermae with naked seeds.

Order - Rosales - the rose order including the
    rose family with its related families like
    Leguminosae (Legumes).

Family - Rosaceae - the rose family made up of
    roses, apples, etc. Families are usually
    named from some outstanding genus and al-
    most always end in -aceae.

8

Genus - Rosa - the various kinds of roses. As
it happens this genus gave the name to the
family and order.

Species - cinnamomea - the Cinnamon Rose.

Instead of writing out all the above names for
this rose we use only the last two, Rosa cinnamomea
Linnaeus, this constituting what is called the
"scientific, botanical or technical" name of the
plant. Anyone interested in such a name would know
of course that the genus Rosa belongs in the Rosaceae
family, and that this family belongs in the Order
Rosales etc. The author's name (Linnaeus or abbreviated to L.) is a part of the name and ought to be
included especially when absolute accuracy is necessary. Sometimes two people had a hand in naming a
plant and we have a double citation, one of the names
appearing in parenthesis. An example would be Rosa
arkansana variety suffulta (Greene) Cockerell. This
new plant was discovered by Greene and considered by
him to be a new species, Rosa suffulta Greene. But
Cockerell placed it as a variety of Rosa arkansana
Porter, and made a new combination but gave Greene
credit for naming the plant first by placing his name
in parenthesis as indicated.

Another example would be the name of our peach,
Prunus persica (L.) Batsch. The grand old Swedish
botanist Linnaeus gave it the name Amygdalus persica
L. way back in 1753. But Batsch later decided that
the peach belonged in with the plums and cherries in
the genus Prunus and made the transfer but gave
Linnaeus credit in parenthesis for first giving the
plant its valid specific name.

HOW GENERIC AND SPECIFIC NAMES ORIGINATE.

It should be of interest to notice how these
scientific names originate. Such a procedure not
only gives a general understanding of the whole subject but also may help us in remembering many of
them should this ever become necessary. As we will
see they are not just a string of meaningless syl-
lables. The following are the most common ways that
scientific names come about.

1. Generic names.

  a. In honor of some man, as Lobelia (the lobelias) named for Matthias de l'Obel.
  b. The classical name of the plant, as Verbascum (the mulleins) an old Latin name.
  c. A character of the group as Penstemon (the beard-tongues) from pente - five and stemon - meaning stamen.

2. Specific names.

  a. In honor of a man - Rosa woodsii Lindl. Named for Joseph Wood. Many botanists prefer to start such specific names with a capital letter.
  b. An old classical name - Verbascum thapsus L. - "Thapsus" is a classical name, from ancient Thapsus.
  c. A generic name once used and adapted as a specific name - Saponaria vaccaria L. "Vaccaria" is the old generic name, from "vacca" or cow. Many botanists capitalize the initial letter in such names.
  d. After a locality - Rosa carolina L. from Carolina.
  e. After some characteristic of the species. Rosa cinnamomea L. with fragrance of cinnamon.

CATEGORIES BELOW THE SPECIES.

  Botanists have recognized certain strains of plants that stand out by themselves but are not sufficiently distinctive to be considered separate and independent species. Several terminologies have been proposed for these subgroups. A common one is as follows.

  1. Varieties. Rosa carolina var. grandiflora (Baker) Rehd. This would be the "large flowered" type of Rosa carolina L. Often such varieties have a separate geographical range. These taxonomic varieties are not to be confused with the horticultural "varieties" of cultivated plants.

10

2. **Forma.** *Saxifraga oppositifolia* forma
albiflora (Lange) Fernald. This would be
the white flowered type of *Saxifraga
oppositifolia* L. which usually has lilac or
violet flowers. It is used for a minor
varient, usually represented by a few unusual individuals scattered among the normal
ones. The botanist's "forma" would corre-
spond rather closely to the horticulturist's
"variety". However, another group of
botanists use the term "subspecies" with
about the same meaning as "variety" in the
preceding outline. For example, *Erigeron
glabellus* subspecies *pubescens* (Hook.)
Cronquist would indicate a major subdivision
of the species. This is not so confusing
but unfortunately such workers use "variety"
about as "forma" was used in the first outline. *Erigeron belliastrum* var. *robustus*
Cronquist would be the robust minor varient
of the species. This does not especially
concern the ordinary student who uses one
manual only. It is hoped that uniformity
in the nomenclature of these subspecific
entities will be attained in the near
future.

The technical names of plants are written in
Latin but often translated from Greek into that
language. However, such names are not pronounced according to the rules used in courses in Latin - at
least in the United States. Instead they are given
an English swing. Some manuals give suggestions on
proper pronunciation but you can expect to find a
great deal of variation among botanists in this respect.

Chapter III

COMMON NAMES AND SCIENTIFIC NAMES

In the preceding chapter we learned that the generic and specific name (with author or authors) constitute the scientific name of the plant. But so called "common names" for certain species have come into more or less general use, especially if the plant is widespread or has some particular interest. "Rose" happens to be the common name of the genus Rosa. Many people will not use any but a common name and may even resent hearing the botanical name. It is important that a student understands the situation concerning plant names exactly, especially if he ever happens to have close contact with the public in general.

VALUES OF COMMON NAMES.

1. They are the only names known and familiar to most people.

2. They are usually simple and relatively easy to remember, usually using words in common use. For example, "Windflower, Mayflower".

3. They are often remarkably descriptive of the plant. For example such names as "Bleeding Heart, Bluebell, Jack-in-the-Pulpit and Dutchman's Breeches", certainly call to mind in clever fashion the appearance of the plants so designated.

WEAKNESSES OF COMMON NAMES.

1. The meaning is clear in only one language.

2. The same plant may have many common names, sometimes by different people in the same area, sometimes in different parts of the country. For example an early spring flower, Pulsatilla ludoviciana (Nutt.) Heller, is known in the writer's circle of acquaintances as both "March Anemone" and "Pasque Flower". A lovely flower of the Rocky Mountain area, Calochortus nuttallii Torr.

is known in Colorado as "Mariposa Lily" but in Utah it has been selected as their state flower under the name of "Sego Lily". Who is to say which is right and which is wrong?

3. The same common name may apply to several plants, both in the same area or in different parts of the country. Names like Mayflower, Bluebell, Soft Maple, Pine and Syringa really have no specific meaning. Even the Irish term "Shamrock" seems to be used for several different species of plants.

4. Common names may actually be ridiculous. For example, "Pineapple" which is not in any way related to either pines or apples "Pepper grass" which is neither a grass or related to pepper, and "Dandelion" which translates "tooth of a lion". Such names do seem inappropriate and may offend some people's sense of logic.

5. Common names have no method or law about them. They rest only on the insecure foundation of general use. Therefore a particular name cannot be called correct and another incorrect. Rather recently an attempt was made to get some order into the situation especially as it applies to horticultural plants. A book called "Standardized Plant Names" was assembled by a committee, listing scientific names followed by a recommended common name. Although a step in the right direction this publication is still incomplete. It has been criticized as being hurriedly assembled and for one reason or another it is not followed by most botanists.

VALUE OF SCIENTIFIC NAMES.

1. They are organized and evaluated according to a definite system of laws and rules. These are passed by an International Congress of Botanical Nomenclature. Several of these conventions have met in the last century, the last one at Paris, France in 1954.

13

At the present time practically all taxonomists work according to these rules.

2. A plant widely distributed over the world has the same valid scientific name. Not only that but the name is written the same in any country. Reprints of articles written in Japanese for example, have the plant names listed in Roman type and the reader may discover that many of the genera and even some of the species are familiar to him.

3. A plant can have only one valid name. It may have picked up several names along the way but all but the correct one are called "synonyms".

4. Only one plant may have this valid name. Should this name be used through error for a different plant then we call it a "homonym". For example if a new rose species was discovered and named Rosa cinnamomea, this would be an invalid homonym since the name had already been properly used.

5. A scientific name is very often descriptive of the plant, as Penstemon unilateralis Rydb. This means a plant with one-sided flowers (unilateralis) belonging to a group with 5 stamens (Penstemon). Or the name may be of interest historically. In any case it has some kind of meaning providing of course one is familiar with the simple Latin used.

POSSIBLE WEAKNESSES OF SCIENTIFIC NAMES.

1. Only recently has nomenclature been uniform in this country. For many years, up to about 1930, American botanists were using two sets of rules - some followed the International Rules, others the so-called American Rules. This resulted in the different selection of the valid name for about one out of eight cases. Unfortunately some of the existing manuals for plant identification were written in the period before 1930.

14

2. Any law or rule may result in injustice and
    confusion in specific cases. This does not
    mean that we must at once do away with law
    and order entirely.

3. Changes in old familiar names may occur.
    These are disconcerting and irritating.
    But one of the rules of nomenclature is that
    the first name lawfully created must be the
    valid name. This is called the "law of
    priority", surely no one would quarrel with
    its principle. Unfortunately some plant
    known for years by a botanical name may be
    found to have been named earlier. We must
    then abandon the familiar name for an un-
    familiar one even though we do not wish to
    do so. It would hardly do to allow a bot-
    anist to make exceptions in certain cases
    and follow the rules in others. The law
    itself would soon come to be meaningless.

4. In a few cases the meaning and logic is
    lost. For example, Linnaeus named 2
    species of Convallaria with 2 and 3 leaves
    on the stem respectively as Convallaria
    bifolia L. and C. trifolia L. Later on
    Greene decided these species belonged to the
    genus Unifolium and used the first recorded
    specific name. This made the rather start-
    ling and certainly illogical combinations,
    Unifolium bifolium (L.) Greene and
    Unifolium trifolium (L.) Greene, the 2-
    leaved and 3-leaved species of a 1-leaved
    genus! Such cases are of course the ex-
    ceptions rather than the rule.

    Then again many scientific names, such as
    those named for some little known man or
    some unfamiliar geographical area may have
    no meaning at all for the average student
    and must be learned by rote.

5. Scientific names are often very long and
    made up of unusual and unfamiliar syllables.
    This makes it hard for people not trained
    in classical languages to remember them.
    However, such names as Geranium, Rhodo-
    dendron and Chrysanthemum are rather long
    generic names but because they have come
    into general use as common names they do

not seem particularly difficult for most of us. Some people just will not listen to technical names and may consider you "high hat" or pedantic if you use them, often suspecting you of making an ostentatious display of knowledge.

SUGGESTED COMPROMISE.

If you are talking to people not familiar with scientific names then you must use their language. But take time to explain the situation to them and avoid misunderstandings. For example, they may know the plant by another name than the one you use, and may either privately suspect your identification or attempt to argue the matter with you publicly. Of course it is folly to argue with anyone on the cor- rectness of a common name.

Sometimes it may be judicious to give several common names for the plant but this may often be merely confusing. One can say, "This plant goes by several names but 'Mariposa Lily' seems to be the one more commonly used around here".

If a plant is brought to you for determination it is wise to write down the common and scientific name on a card and hand it to the inquirer. Some- times such names get into print or at least are passed around by word of mouth. The scientific name will allow other botanists to know exactly what plant it was you checked.

All records of vegetation and all published lists in scientific articles should be in botanical terminology. Even popular articles should have the scientific name of the plant or plants listed some- where. The writer has read scores of articles, pamphlets and bulletins written about some plant, the exact species of which could not be accurately ascertained from the context.

Many beginners learn the common names of plants and then append to that name the scientific one. If they continue to study plants the process is grad- ually reversed and they will reason thus, "This plant is a species of Calochortus, oh yes, commonly called Mariposa Lily".

Chapter IV

TERMS RELATIVE TO THE FLOWER

PARTS OF A FLOWER.

The flower is the structure most commonly used in classifying and identifying plants. A pear tree (Pyrus sp.), a climbing rose (Rosa sp.) and an herbaceous strawberry (Fragaria sp.) are placed by most botanists in the same family, not because of similarities in general appearance but because their flowers bear a common stamp of the rose family.

Below is a diagram of a typical flower with the parts labeled. Actually the "drawing" is a hypothetical longitudinal section through the flower, with only 2 stamens, 2 petals and 2 sepals shown at the sides. Of course in an actual flower several to many of these structures are usually present in a whorl or circle. Several other diagrams of this nature follow. Almost any possible modification, variation or combination can occur. Fig. 2.

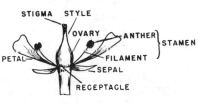

Fig. 2.

FLOWERS IN GENERAL.

1. Anthesis. The period during which the flower parts are open and receptive for pollination.

2. Ephemeral. Lasting for a short time, usually for one day or less.

3. Caducous. Falling off unusually early as compared with similar structures on other plants.

4. Fugacious. Falling off or fading unusually early. About the same as caducous.

5. Marcescent. Withering but persisting and not falling off readily.

17

6. **Many.** Eleven or more. Same as numerous. Ordinarily the exact number above 11 has no great taxonomic significance.

7. **Complete and Incomplete.** A complete flower has sepals, petals, stamens and pistils present, an incomplete flower lacks one or more of these four parts. The diagrams are hypothetical longitudinal sections of a flower. Fig. 3 and Fig. 4.

COMPLETE FLOWER
Fig. 3.

INCOMPLETE FLOWERS
Fig. 4.

8. **Perfect** (bisexual or hermaphroditic) and **Imperfect** (unisexual). A perfect flower has both stamens and pistils (may or may not have other parts) but an imperfect flower lacks either stamens or pistils. Each diagram shows a longitudinal section of the flower. Fig. 5 and Fig. 6.

PERFECT FLOWERS
Fig. 5.

IMPERFECT FLOWERS
Fig. 6.

18

9. Staminate and pistillate flowers. A staminate
flower lacks a pistil or pistils; a pistillate
flower lacks stamens. Petals and sepals may be
present or absent.

10. Monoecious. Flowers imperfect (unisexual) with
the staminate and pistillate ones on the same
plant. An example would be corn (or maize), the
"tassel" with staminate flowers, the "ear" with
pistillate flowers.

11. Dioecious. Flowers imperfect (unisexual) with
the staminate flowers on one plant, the pistillate flowers on another. An example would be a
cottonwood tree. Such dioecious plants are
often referred to as "male" and "female" individuals.

12. Polygamous. Used by most manuals to mean perfect (bisexual) and imperfect (unisexual)
flowers on the same or on different individual
plants. The imperfect flowers in such cases are
usually staminate.

13. Pedicel. The stalk
to an individual
flower in an inflores-
cence. Compare
peduncle. Fig. 7.

14. Peduncle. The stalk
to an inflorescence
or to a solitary
flower (like a tulip).
See Figure 7 also.
Fig. 8.

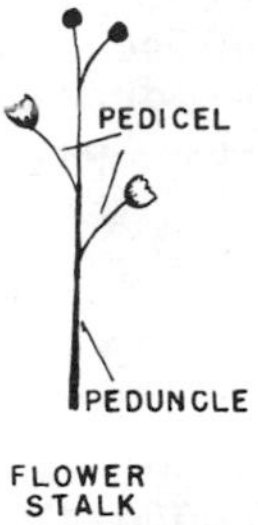

PEDICEL

PEDUNCLE

PEDUNCLE

FLOWER
STALK

FLOWER STALK

Fig. 7. 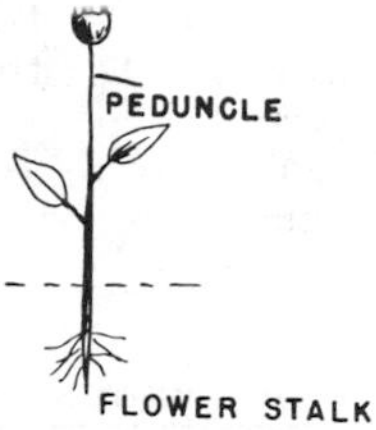   Fig. 8.

15. Bract. A reduced or modified leaf
near a flower or an inflorescence.
Very small bracts may be called
bractlets. Fig. 9.

BRACT

Fig. 9.

16. Involucre. A whorl of distinct or united leaves or bracts subtending (associated with) a flower or an inflorescence. When the involucre appears to be made up of leaves then these are distinctly different in some way from the ordinary leaves below. Fig. 10.

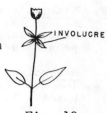

Fig. 10.

17. Petaloid. Resembling a petal in some way, usually colored other than green. Often used for sepals or bracts.

INSERTION OF PARTS.

1. Hypogynous flower. A flower with sepals and petals (when all are present) attached under the ovary. A longitudinal diagram is given for this and the following three types. Fig. 11.

HYPOGYNOUS FLOWER
Fig. 11.

2. Epigynous flower. The other flower parts arise from the summit of an inferior ovary or appear to do so. Fig. 12.

EPIGYNOUS FLOWER
Fig. 12.

3. Perigynous flower. Borne or arising from around the ovary. Where the stamens or petals (or both) are borne on the edge of a cup-shaped calyx tube or hypanthium. The term "perigynous" is more logically used to describe the insertion of stamens (stamens perigynous) or petals (petals perigynous) rather than applied to the flower as a whole. Fig. 13.

PERIGYNOUS FLOWER
Fig. 13.

4. Ovary partly inferior. Fig. 14.

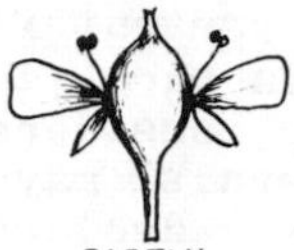

PARTLY
INFERIOR
OVARY

Fig. 14.

UNION OF PARTS.

1. Connate or distinct. "Connate" means the union
    of like parts (such as petal united to petal);
    "distinct" means like parts not united.

2. Adnate or free. "Adnate" means union of unlike
    parts (as calyx tube to ovary); "free" means un-
    like parts not united.

3. Connivent. Parts in close contact but not act-
    ually united by tissue.

ARRANGEMENT OF PARTS.

1. Imbricate. Partly overlapping DIAGRAM OF A FLOWER
    like shingles on a roof,
    either laterally or vertically.
    One drawing shows the ver-
    tical overlapping, the other
    shows the lateral overlapping
    in cross-section. Fig. 15.

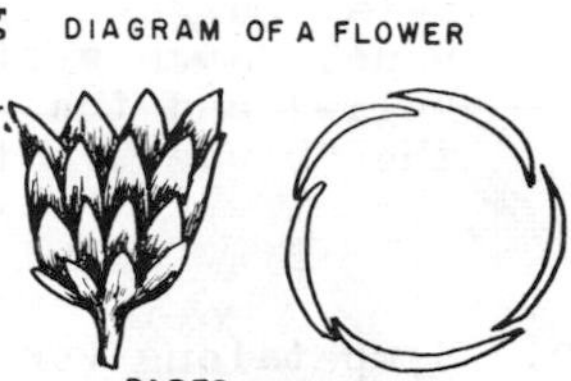

PARTS IMBRICATED

Fig. 15.

2. Valvate. Where the parts come to-
    gether edge to edge but not over-
    lapping. The drawing shows the parts
    in cross-section, like sepals in a
    bud, the structures inside not shown.
    Fig. 16.

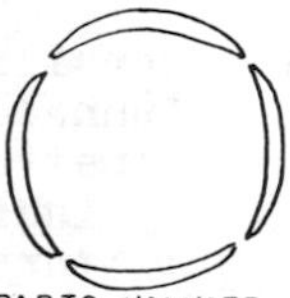

PARTS VALVATE

Fig. 16.

CALYX.

    This is usually green and protects or encloses
the petals in the bud. The calyx may be modified or
absent entirely. When only one whorl of the perianth

21

is present it is always considered to be the calyx
even when it is colored (the petals in such a case
are considered to be lacking). The calyx segments
(sepals) may be persistent as in apple or caducous
(very deciduous) as in the bloodroot or prickly
poppy.

COROLLA.

This is usually colored and conspicuous. The
corolla segments (petals) may be caducous as in the
flax, or persistent.

1. Polypetalous. Petals distinct, not
    united at all to each other. One
    would expect this word to mean "many
    petals" but this is not the case.
    Fig. 17.

POLYPETALOUS
COROLLA
Fig. 17.

2. Claw and blade. Often a single
    petal narrows to a stalk-like
    base. Such a stalk is called a
    "claw" and the expanded portion
    the "blade". Fig. 18.

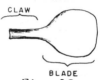

Fig. 18.

3. Sympetalous (or gamopetalous). Petals united at
    least at the base. Such a corolla may have 3
    more or less definite parts as shown on the draw-
    ing of a funnelform corolla. (Fig. 19.)

4. Corolla funnelform. Shaped like a
    funnel. Sympetalous corollas are
    sometimes divided into a rather
    cylindrical base called a "tube",
    a "throat" at the orifice of the
    tube and a "limb" where the lobes
    occur. But often this is obscure.
    Fig. 19.

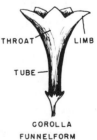

COROLLA
FUNNELFORM
Fig. 19.

5. Corolla rotate. The tube is short and the throat and limb are abruptly flaring. Fig. 20.

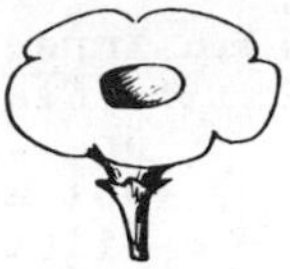

COROLLA
ROTATE
Fig. 20.

6. Corolla campanulate. Bell-shaped. Such flowers may be erect but often hang down as in the drawing. Fig. 21.

COROLLA
CAMPANULATE
Fig. 21.

7. Corolla salverform. With a long tube and abruptly flaring throat and limb. The phlox is an excellent example. Fig. 22.

COROLLA
SALVERFORM
Fig. 22.

8. Corolla cylindrical. Shaped like a cylinder, the sides nearly or quite parallel. This shape is not common. Fig. 23.

COROLLA
CYLINDRICAL
Fig. 23.

9. Regular flower (Actinomorphic). The individual parts of one whorl (like the petals) are all alike. The flower has a radial type of symmetry. Fig. 24.

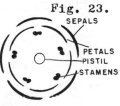

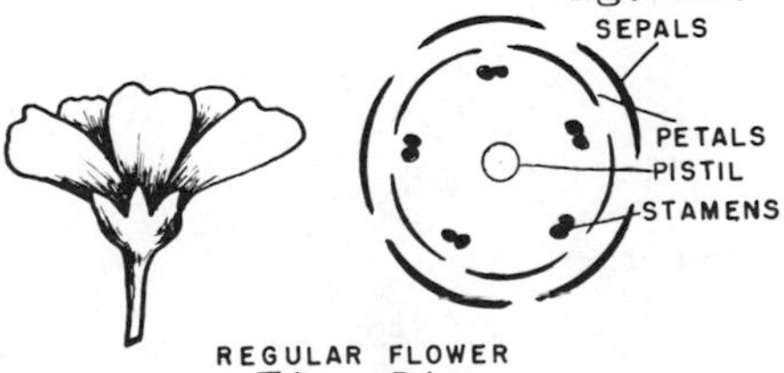

SEPALS
PETALS
PISTIL
STAMENS

REGULAR FLOWER
Fig. 24.

23

10. Irregular flower (Zygomorphic).
A flower in which the parts of
one whorl (like the petals) are
not alike. The flower has
bilateral symmetry, and may be
2-lipped in its extreme form as
in the figure. Fig. 25.

IRREGULAR FLOWER
Fig. 25.

11. Spur. An elongated structure,
containing nectar, shaped something like the spur of a fight-
ing cock. This spur may be
part of a sepal (as in the drawing) or of a petal. Fig. 26.

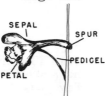

Fig. 26.

12. Gland. This is a secreting surface or structure, or an appendage having the general appearance
of such an organ. Glands vary
greatly in appearance and general
character. They can be found on
other structures but are often associated with petals. Fig. 27.

PETAL WITH GLAND
Fig. 27.

STAMENS.

1. Anther and filament. The anther is
the pollen producing portion, the
filament is the stalk to the anther.
Fig. 28.

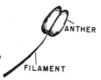

STAMEN
Fig. 28.

2. Anthers basifixed. Attached by one end
to the filament. Fig. 29.

BASIFIXED
ANTHER
Fig. 29.

24

3. Anthers versatile. Attached to the filament at or near the middle with a "teeter totter" effect. Compare basifixed (Fig. 29).

4. Stamens monadelphous. The stamens are more or less united in one general structure. Fig. 30.

MONADELPHOUS
STAMENS
Fig. 30.

5. Stamens diadelphous. The stamens united in 2 sets. A common example would be most legume flowers, in two sets of 9 and 1 as in the Figure 31.

DIADELPHOUS
STAMENS
Fig. 31.

6. Stamens didynamous. Stamens in 2 sets of unequal length. In the drawing a sympetalous corolla has been split down one side and rolled open; the stamens are inserted on the corolla. Fig. 32.

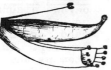

DIDYNAMOUS
STAMENS
Fig. 32.

7. Stamens tetradynamous. Stamens in 2 sets with 4 longer and 2 shorter. Characteristic of the Cruciferae or Mustard family. In the drawing the sepals and petals are omitted. Fig. 33.

TETRADYNAMOUS
STAMENS
Fig. 33.

25

8. Staminode (staminodium). A sterile
    stamen, for example one lacking an
    anther or a structure resembling
    one, and borne with the stamens.
    The drawing shows 4 ordinary stamens
    and one sterile one (staminode).
    The sepals and petals are omitted.
    Fig. 34.

STERILE STAMEN

STAMINODE

Fig. 34.

9. Stamen exserted. Protruding
    beyond a surrounding organ,
    usually the corolla. Can be
    used for any 2 structures,
    however. In the drawings the
    stamens and style are ex-
    serted from the corolla.
    Fig. 35. and Fig. 36.

STYLE EXSERTED
Fig. 35.

STAMENS EXSERTED
Fig. 36.

10. Stamens included. Not protruding
    beyond the surrounding structure.
    The corolla in the drawing has
    been split and partially flattened
    out. Fig. 37.

STAMENS
INCLUDED
Fig. 37.

PISTIL.

There may be one, several or many
pistils to a flower. Usually one can make
out 3 different parts to a pistil, the
stigma, style and ovary. The stigma receives the pollen grains and is often hairy,
roughened or sticky. The ovary bears the
ovules. Fig. 38.

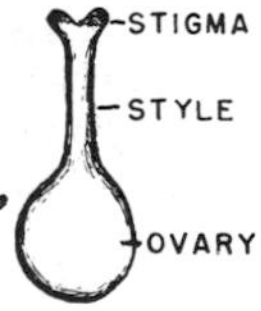

STIGMA

STYLE

OVARY

PISTIL
Fig. 38.

1. Locule. A cell or compartment to an ovary, best
    seen in cross-section. It is not an empty space
    but filled with the attached ovules. The number
    of locules to an ovary has to be ascertained in
    almost every case. This may be somewhat diffi-
    cult to do in a small pistil. The following

26

suggestions may aid in acquiring the special
little knack of sectioning ovaries.

A. Keep the blade very sharp. Many botanists
    use single edge safety razor blades, discard-
    ing the dull ones.

B. Draw the blade through the center of the
    ovary using a diagonal stroke such as a man
    may use in shaving with a straight edge
    razor. Fig. 39.

Fig. 39.

C. Cut a thin slice and let it dry for a minute
    or two. The succulent ovules will usually
    shrink and the details of the cells will be
    plainer.

D. Or cut the ovary in upper and lower halves.
    Pick out the ovules with a needle from one
    of the cut surfaces. This will show up the
    structural details within. Rotating the
    half ovary with some pressure may squeeze
    out the still attached ovules and give the
    same effect.

E. Try to find a partly developed fruit. An
    ovary in its enlargement to the fruit or-
    dinarily does not change in its internal
    structure. The parts are merely larger and
    easier to study.

2. Septum. This is the wall
    between the locules. At
    its outer limits it runs in-
    to the ovary wall. Fig. 40.

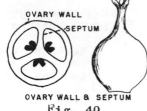

OVARY WALL & SEPTUM
Fig. 40.

3. Ovary wall. The outer wall of the ovary. (Fig.
    40.)

4. Placentae. The place or part of an ovary where
    the ovules are attached. Four types of placen-
    tation are most common.

    A. Parietal. Ovules at-
        tached at the outer wall
        of the ovary which is al-
        most always one-celled.
        The drawings include a
        cross-section of the
        ovary. Fig. 41.

3 PARIETAL PLACENTAE
Fig. 41.

    B. Axile. Ovary 2- or more-
        celled with the ovules at-
        tached at the center. Each
        drawing shows a cross-
        section of an ovary.
        Fig. 42.

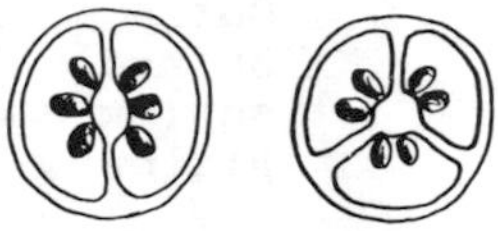

AXILE PLACENTAE
Fig. 42.

    C. Basal. The ovules attached at the
        base of the one-celled ovary. The
        drawing shows an ovary in longi-
        tudinal section with one ovule.
        Fig. 43.

BASAL
PLACENTA
Fig. 43.

28

D. Free-central. The ovules
borne on a central column a-
rising from the base of a one-
celled ovary. This central
column may be made up (at
least in part) of several
fused placentae. A cross-
section of the ovary is shown
in the drawing to the right.
Fig. 44.

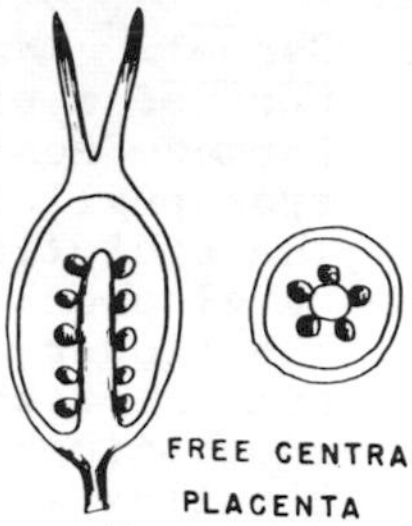

FREE CENTRAL
PLACENTA
Fig. 44.

5. Sporophyll. A spore bearing leaf
in the non-flowering plants.
Sepals and petals are thought to
be sterile sporophylls, stamens
and pistils are modified sporophylls. The drawing suggests how
a sporophyll could have rolled up
to form an anther in the evolutionary development of a stamen.
Fig. 45.

SPOROPHYLL
COMPARED TO ANTHER
Fig. 45.

The following drawing
indicates how a sporophyll
could have rolled up to
form a pistil. Such a
pistil would have one carpel only. Fig. 46.

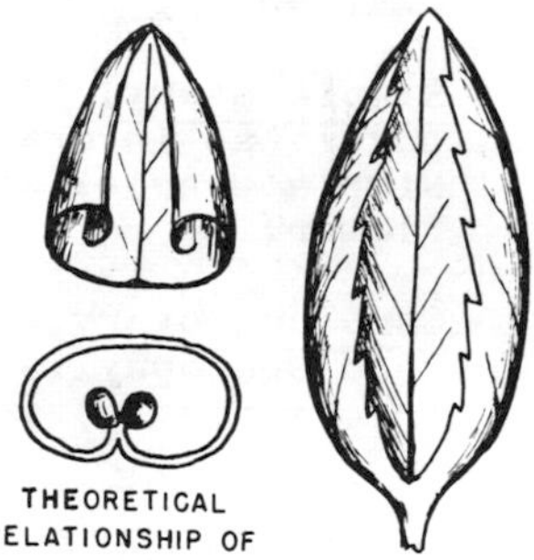

THEORETICAL
RELATIONSHIP OF
SPOROPHYLL TO   SPOROPHYLL
OVARY   ROLLING IN
Fig. 46.
Part 1   Part 2

6. Carpel. That part of a pistil formed from one sporophyll in the evolutionary development of the flower. The number of carpels is obtained by counting the stigma lobes, the styles, the locules and the placentae. The highest number will be the number of carpels. (Various degrees of fusion occur.) However, some placentae are double or paired as in Fig. 47 but are still counted as one. Fig. 47 and Fig. 48.

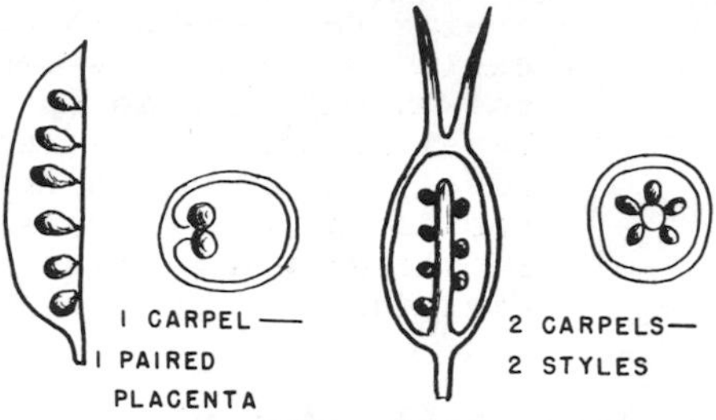

I CARPEL—
I PAIRED PLACENTA

2 CARPELS—
2 STYLES

Fig. 47.

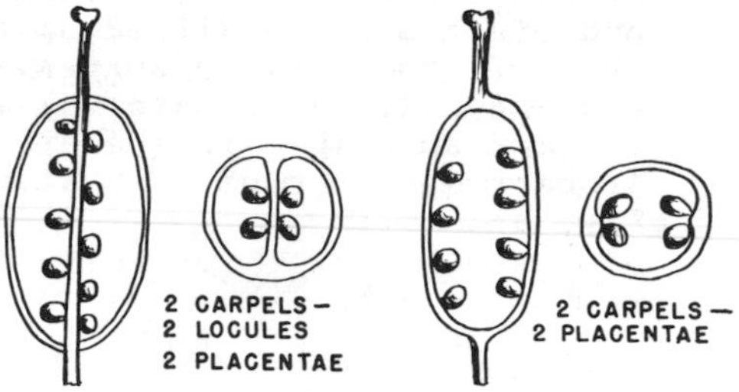

2 CARPELS—
2 LOCULES
2 PLACENTAE

2 CARPELS—
2 PLACENTAE

Fig. 48.

7. Simple ovary. An ovary formed from one sporophyll, as in drawing number 47 (left figure). Simple ovaries are often more than one to a flower.

8. Compound ovary. An ovary formed from two or more sporophylls, as in drawing number 47 (right figure) and 48 (both figures).

30

Chapter V

TERMS RELATIVE TO THE INFLORESCENCE

Often flowers are grouped in variously arranged
clusters called inflorescences. The more common
terms relative to these inflorescences are discussed
below.

1. Indeterminate (racemose or centrifugal). In
   this type the young flowers (or even primordial
   tissue) are at the end of the main axis, or in
   the case of the umbel in the center, while the
   older flowers are below or to the outside. In
   such an inflorescence it is sometimes possible
   to find buds at the top, mature flowers at the
   middle and fruit at the base of the main axis.
   It is called "indeterminate" because it is
   theoretically possible for such an inflorescence
   to continue developing new flowers at the tip
   for an indeterminate length of time. Actually
   in most cases development stops rather soon.

2. Determinate (cymose or centripetal). Here the
   oldest flower is at the end of the main axis with
   the younger flowers arising from below. Sometimes when the rachis is non-existent, as in an
   unusual umbel, the central flowers may be older
   with the outer flowers younger. Such a case
   would be a special type of "determinate" inflorescence. The cyme is the only example of this
   type.

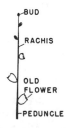

3. Spike. An indeterminate type of inflorescence with the flowers sessile
   along the main axis (rachis).
   Fig. 49.

SPIKE
Fig. 49.

31

4. Raceme. An indeterminate type of inflorescence with the flowers single on pedicels arranged along an elongated rachis. When the pedicels are very short and the flowers crowded the raceme resembles a spike at first glance and is called "spike-like". Fig. 50.

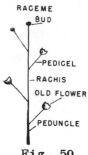

Fig. 50.

5. Panicle. An indeterminate type of inflorescence with 2 or more flowers on each branch, these arranged on an elongated axis (usually called a "rachis" or a "main axis"). Fig. 51.

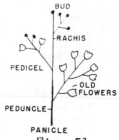

Fig. 51.

6. Cormyb. An indeterminate flat-topped inflorescence. It is essentially a raceme with the lower pedicels elongated and the rachis more or less shortened. Fig. 52.

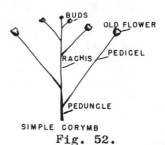

Fig. 52.

    A corymb can be compound, with several corymb-like clusters, these in turn crowded into a larger, collective corymb. Fig. 53.

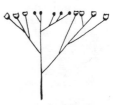

COMPOUND CORYMB

Fig. 53.

32

7. Umbel. An indetermin-
ate type of flat-topped
or orbicular inflores-
cence with the rachis
non-existent. Fig. 54
and Fig. 55.

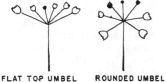

FLAT TOP UMBEL   ROUNDED UMBEL
Fig. 54.   Fig. 55.

Umbels can be compound as in
Fig. 56.

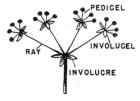

PEDICEL

INVOLUCEL

RAY

INVOLUCRE

COMPOUND UMBEL
Fig. 56.

8. Head. A dense
cluster of usually
indeterminate, ses-
sile or nearly sessile
flowers (or fruits)
on a very short axis.
It is used especially
for the involucrate
inflorescence in the
Compositae family.
Fig. 57 and Fig. 58.

CLOVER   SUNFLOWER
HEAD   HEAD
Fig. 57.   Fig. 58.

Figure 59 is a longitud-
inal section of Figure
58.

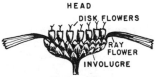

HEAD
DISK FLOWERS

RAY
FLOWER

INVOLUCRE

Fig. 59.

33

9. Cyme. A determin-
   ate inflorescence.
   It may be of vari-
   ous shapes or de-
   grees of branching
   but the oldest
   flower is always on
   the end of the
   branch. Fig. 60.

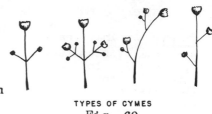

TYPES OF CYMES
Fig. 60.

10. Glomerule. A general term for a densely packed
    cluster of flowers.

11. Scorpioid. An inflorescence of
    one-sided flowers coiled at the
    apex like the tail of a scorpion.
    Fig. 61.

SCORPIOID RACEME
Fig. 61.

12. Thyrse. A cylindrical or ovoid-
    pyramidal, usually densely flowered
    panicle on the order of a cluster
    of grapes or a lilac inflorescence.
    Fig. 62.

THYRSE
Fig. 62.

13. Spadix. A spike with a thick
    and fleshy central axis, usually
    densely flowered with imperfect
    flowers. Such an inflorescence
    is often subtended by a large
    bract called a spathe. Fig. 63.

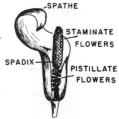

SPATHE
STAMINATE
FLOWERS
SPADIX
PISTILLATE
FLOWERS

SPADIX & SPATHE
Fig. 63.

34

14. Ament or catkin. A spike or spike-like inflorescence made up of unisexual flowers. Willows, poplars and cottonwoods are plants bearing aments. Fig. 64.

AMENT
OR CATKIN
Fig. 64.

15. Solitary. Flowers borne singly, not in clusters. These may be terminal or axillary as indicated in the drawing. Fig. 65.

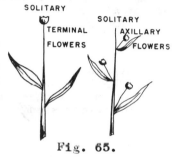

SOLITARY
TERMINAL
FLOWERS

SOLITARY
AXILLARY
FLOWERS

Fig. 65.

16. Combinations. Sometimes the flowers are borne in inflorescences whose general nature is one type but the individual parts are of another. A combination term may be necessary like the one figured. Fig. 66.

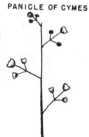

PANICLE OF CYMES

Fig. 66.

Chapter VI

TERMS RELATIVE TO UNDERGROUND PARTS

The specific and even the generic differences of
plants are often based on underground characters.
Every specimen of a herbaceous plant ought to indicate either by the actual material or by notes on
the label any underground character that might be of
value in identifying material in that particular
group. Some characteristic structures of that type
are as follows.

1. Taproot. A thick tapering root, on the
    order of a beet or carrot root. A tap-
    root may be thick as in the drawing or
    relatively slender. Fig. 67.

TAP ROOT
Fig. 67.

2. Tuber. A thickened subterranean stem
    typically with numerous buds (eyes)
    like a potato. Fig. 68.

TUBER
Fig. 68.

3. Bulb. A subterranean bud having fleshy
    scales like an onion. The drawing
    shows the bulb in longitudinal section.
    Fig. 69.

BULB
Fig. 69.

4. Corm. A vertical, thickened, solid underground stem such as borne by a crocus or gladiolus. Fig. 70.

CORM
(SOLID CENTER)
Fig. 70.

5. Rhizome. A prostrate more or less horizontally elongated stem growing partly or completely beneath the surface of the ground, usually rooting at the nodes and becoming upcurved at the apex. Sometimes called a "rootstock". The scales on the drawing are actually modified leaves. Fig. 71.

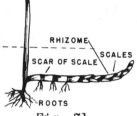

Fig. 71.

6. Annual root. A root that develops with the stem for the season and dies with it at the end of that season. It is seldom much enlarged, has no special food storage structures and usually merges into the stem without a break caused by scars or constrictions. (See perennial root discussion.) The scars of the cotyledons may show as indicated on the drawing and the early leaves may wither or drop leaving scars on the basal part of the stem. Fig. 72.

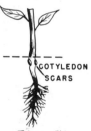

Fig. 72.

7. Perennial root. One that lives over winter and initiates the stem growth from buds. In a woody plant these buds are borne above the ground, in a herbaceous perennial plant they are produced at or near the ground level. Such a root must be large enough to store enough food to start the new growth in the spring. Fig. 73.

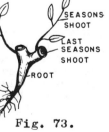

Fig. 73.

37

Sometimes perennial roots become horizontally elongated and
spread the plant on the order of
rhizomes, but rhizomes have reduced leaves (scales) or scars
where the scales dropped away.
True roots lack such structures.
Fig. 74.

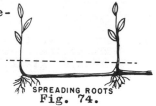

SPREADING ROOTS
Fig. 74.

8. Annual and perennial plants.

(1) Woody plants are always perennial ones.

(2) Plants with special organs for food storage
such as tubers, bulbs, corms, rhizomes,
etc., are perennial.

(3) Plants with large roots are usually perennial.

(4) Plants with remnants of last year's stem
attached to the crown or roots are perennial plants (See Fig. 73). Be careful your
specimen isn't an annual plant late in the
season where the early stem has been cut
off. In such a case this old stem may by
contrast look old and weathered but the new
sprouts from near the base will be green
and fresh looking.

(5) Plants with enlarged crowns near the ground
level, these having a series of scars or
constrictions as they enter up into the
stem, are perennials. The buds on the
crown send up the new stems and a "break"
is almost always apparent where these develop.

An excellent way to develop this concept is to
check the annual or perennial character of every
plant identified as it is listed in the manual after
identification, even though that character might not
have been needed in running it through the key. Then
look carefully at the underground parts of the specimen to see how it squares up with the record.

Chapter VII

TERMS RELATIVE TO THE STEM

Only the more common terms are discussed below. The ones relative to the angle of the stem as compared to the horizontal ground level are sometimes loosely used.

1. Caulescent. Having a leafy stem above the ground. The leaves can be any shape or in any arrangement. Fig. 75.

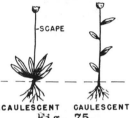

ACAULESCENT   CAULESCENT
Fig. 75.

2. Acaulescent. The leaves clustered at or near the base of the plant. The leafless stalk is called a scape and the plant is described as scapose (having a scape). (See Fig. 75).

3. Strict. A stem rigidly upright. Fig. 76.

STRICT
STEM
Fig. 76.

4. Prostrate. A stem lying flat on the ground, often rooting at the nodes but otherwise not particularly differentiated. Fig. 77.

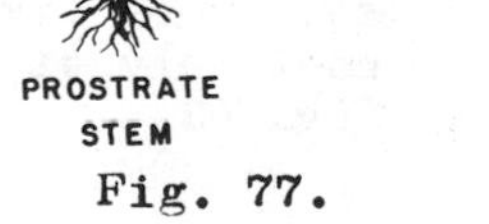

PROSTRATE
STEM
Fig. 77.

5. Decumbent. A stem reclining on
the ground but turned upward near
the end. Fig. 78.

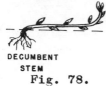

DECUMBENT
STEM
Fig. 78.

6. Ascending. A stem growing obliquely
upward at about a 40 - 60 degree
angle from the horizontal, often
curved as shown on the drawing.
Fig. 79.

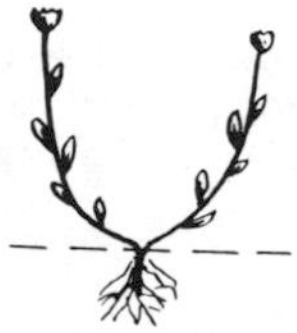

ASCENDING
STEM
Fig. 79.

7. Caespitose. Stems growing in tufts or
rather close clusters. The term is
rather loosely used by some authors.
Also written cespitose. Fig. 80.

CAESPITOSE
STEM
Fig. 80.

8. Stolon. A specialized stem trailing on the ground and rooting at
the nodes. A stolon intergrades
with a prostrate stem. Fig. 81.

STOLON
Fig. 81.

9. Runner. A very slender stolon,
sometimes limited to those that
root only at the apex.
Fig. 82.

RUNNER
Fig. 82.

40

10. Herbaceous. A stem that is not woody like those of trees and shrubs. This term is also used to describe a structure green in color (like the herbage).

11. Woody. A perennial stem that has had time to produce woody tissue, a characteristic bark which is often gray to tan and buds that produce the next season's growth. Sometimes a stem may be woody only at the very base of the plant.

Chapter VIII

TERMS RELATIVE TO THE LEAVES

Differences in leaf characters are often utilized in separating the species of a genus. Sometimes they are used to differentiate between larger units such as the genera in a family. The terms relative to leaf surfaces are treated in Chapter IX.

GENERAL TERMS.

1. Deciduous. Leaves all falling at the end of the growing season or at least withering up and becoming lifeless. Usually a corky layer called the "abscission layer" develops at the base of the petiole, effectively walling off the leaf. When the abscission layer does not split apart, the dead leaf may remain on the stem over part or all the resting period. Fig. 83.

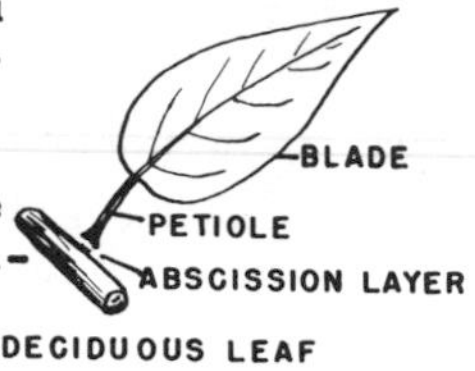

BLADE
PETIOLE
ABSCISSION LAYER
DECIDUOUS LEAF
Fig. 83.

The term "deciduous" is also used for any part that falls away rather early in comparison with the situation for most similar parts.

2. Evergreen. Bearing green leaves throughout the year. Evergreen leaves in most parts of the United States are usually needle-shaped like those on a spruce or pine. Such leaves are not permanent structures of course, and are eventually shed, but some at least remain on the tree all winter.

ARRANGEMENT ON THE STEM.

This refers to the particular way the leaves are inserted on the stem.

42

1. Opposite. Two leaves inserted op-
    posite each other on the stem.
    Fig. 84.

Fig. 84.

2. Alternate. Only one leaf
    inserted at a node.
    Fig. 85.

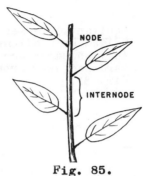

Fig. 85.

3. Whorled (or verticillate).
    With three or more leaves
    inserted at one node.
    Fig. 86.

LEAVES WHORLED
Fig. 86.

4. Radical. The leaves arise from or
    very near the root. When the leaves
    are rather numerous they form what
    is called a "rosette". Fig. 87.

LEAVES RADICAL
Fig. 87.

5. Basal. The leaves tend to crowd down
    toward the base of the stem. The
    term is not very exact but is conven-
    ient. Most basal leaves are es-
    sentially alternate. Fig. 88.

LEAVES BASAL
Fig. 88.

6. Equitant. Leaves that are
    folded or flattened so that
    the two edges are turned to-
    ward and away from the stem.
    Fig. 89.

LEAVES EQUITANT
Fig. 89.

SIMPLE AND COMPOUND LEAVES.

A simple leaf is one with only
one definite segment present between
the stem and the end of the blade.
It may be variously lobed. Fig. 90
and Fig. 91.

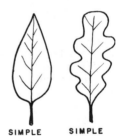

SIMPLE   SIMPLE
Fig. 90.Fig. 91.

A compound
leaf has definite
and distinct seg-
ments (leaflets)
from the stem to
the apex. The
most common types
are pinnately and
palmately compound.
Fig. 92 and Fig.
93.

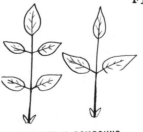

PINNATELY COMPOUND
Fig. 92.

PALMATE
Fig. 93.

44

The common fault in judging simple or compound leaves is to mistake a leaflet for a leaf and consider the leaf rachis to be a stem. However, the majority of compound leaves have a leaflet directly on the end of the rachis. A stem never has a leaf on the end but terminates in a growing point, which may be active or inactive. If this growing area is active then young leaves will be present. Fig. 94 and Fig. 95.

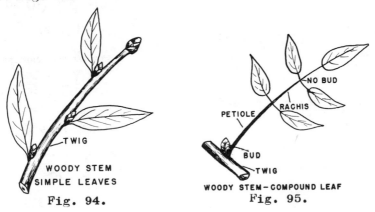

Fig. 94.   Fig. 95.

There may be a bud present at the base of a leaf but never at the base of a leaflet. This is particularly noticeable in plants with woody twigs. The buds may not develop in some herbaceous plants or may produce side branches. Sometimes young shoots are mistakenly considered to be compound leaves especially when the old subtending leaf has withered away. Fig. 96.

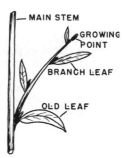

Fig. 96.

1. Decompound. A leaf that is divided once and at least once again. Examples figured can be found under bipinnate, tripinnate and biternate (Figs. 97, 98 and 100).

2. **Bipinnate.** A decompound leaf, pinnately compound with the main divisions once again compound. Fig. 97.

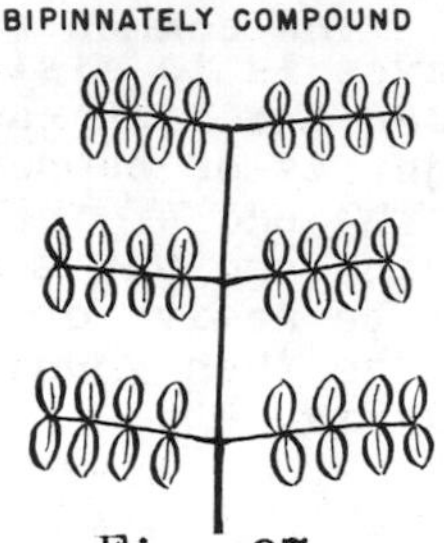

BIPINNATELY COMPOUND

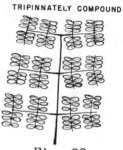

Fig. 97.

TRIPINNATELY COMPOUND

3. **Tripinnate.** A leaf that is three times pinnate. Fig. 98.

Fig. 98.

4. **Ternate.** A compound leaf with 3 equal divisions; palmately compound with 3 leaflets. Fig. 99.

TERNATE
Fig. 99.

5. **Biternate.** A decompound leaf ternate with each main division once again ternate. Fig. 100.

BITERNATE
Fig. 100.

46

6. **Pinnatifid.** A simple leaf but cut very deep in pinnate fashion. Fig. 101.

PINNATIFID
Fig. 101.

7. **Fern leaf.** The fern leaf (frond) has been given special terms as indicated below. The actual stems of our ordinary ferns are at or below the ground level. Fig. 102.

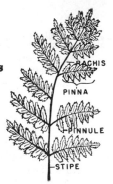

FERN FROND
Fig. 102.

SHAPE.

This is the general outline of the leaf, usually disregarding the tip and base. When the leaf is lobed, the general outline cuts off the lobes and fills in the sinuses. Fig. 103.

OVATE
Fig. 103.

47

1. Needle-shaped (acerose). Very narrow like the leaves of spruce or fir. Such leaves may be terete, quadrangular or flattened in cross-section. Fig. 104.

NEEDLE SHAPED
Fig. 104.

2. Awl-shaped. This is a rather small, narrowly triangular shape like the leaves on some of the Red Cedars or Junipers. Fig. 105.

AWL SHAPED
Fig. 105.

3. Linear. A narrow flat shape with parallel sides. The length is over 4 times the width. Fig. 106.

LINEAR
Fig. 106.

4. Lanceolate. A narrow leaf broadest nearer the base. Fig. 107.

5. Ovate. Egg-shaped and connected at the broader end. Fig. 108.

LANCEOLATE   OVATE
Fig. 107.   Fig. 108.

48

6. Oblanceolate. Lanceolate but connected by the narrower end. Fig. 109.

7. Obovate. Ovate in shape but connected at the narrower end. Fig. 110.

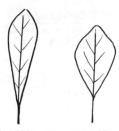

OBLANCEOLATE   OBOVATE
Fig. 109. Fig. 110

8. Oblong. Two to four times longer than wide, the sides parallel or nearly so. Fig. 111.

9. Oval. Broadest at the middle and the width over half the length. This term is loosely used in some manuals. Fig. 112.

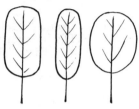

OBLONG   OVAL
Fig. 111.Fig. 112.

10. Elliptic (or elliptical). Broadest at the middle, the ends rather equal. This is another term that is very loosely used but the length is at least twice the width. The drawings show a broadly elliptic and a rather narrowly elliptic leaf. Fig. 113.

ELLIPTIC
Fig. 113.

11. Spatulate. Flattened spoon-shaped, connected at the narrow tapered end. Shaped like the old fashioned "spatula". Fig. 114.

12. Deltoid. Triangular like the Greek letter "Delta". The blade is usually connected to the petiole at the middle of one side. Fig. 115.

SPATULATE   DELTOID
Fig. 114. Fig. 115.

13. Orbicular (round). A flat object of round shape like a dinner plate. A round object in 3 dimensions would be globose.

14. Falcate. Curved and tapering upward like a scimitar, hence asymmetric. Fig. 116.

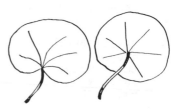

FALCATE
Fig. 116.

15. Reniform. Kidney-shaped, usually connected at the sinus. Fig. 117.

16. Peltate. A leaf, usually broad in shape with the blade connected to the petiole part way in from the margin, giving an opened umbrella-like effect in its extreme form. Fig. 118.

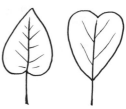

RENIFORM   PELTATE
Fig. 117.   Fig. 118.

17. Cordate. A broadly heart-shaped leaf connected at its broader end. It is really a broadly ovate shape with the base heart-shaped. Fig. 119.

An obcordate leaf would be the same except attached at the narrower end. Fig. 120.

CORDATE   OBCORDATE
Fig. 119. Fig. 120

18. Sagittate. A leaf with arrow-like base, the lobes pointed backward. Fig. 121.

19. Hastate (Halberd-shaped). Shaped like a conventional arrowhead but the basal lobes flaring out. Fig. 122.

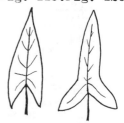

SAGITTATE   HASTATE
Fig. 121. Fig. 122.

50

BASE.

1. Rounded. The sides of the leaf
rounded into the petiole. One
figure has a broadly rounded base,
the other a rather narrowly rounded one. Fig. 123.

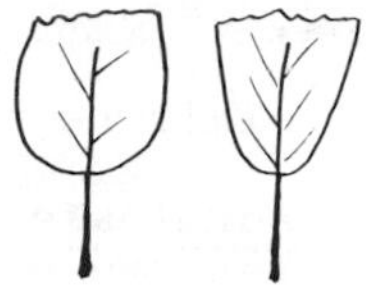

ROUNDED
Fig. 123.

2. Cuneate. Base wedge-shaped, sometimes spoken of as "acute". One
base in the drawings is broadly
cuneate, the other is rather narrowly so. Fig. 124.

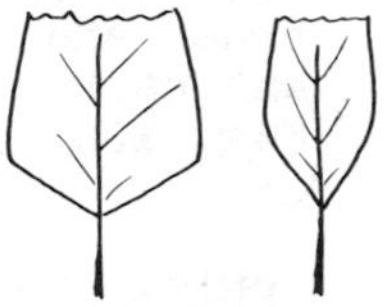

CUNEATE
Fig. 124.

3. Truncate. Base squared
as if cut off by a
straight blade.
Fig. 125.

4. Oblique. The two sides
markedly uneven at base.
Most such leaf bases are
cuneate on one side and
rounded or cordate on the
other. Fig. 126.

TRUNCATE
Fig. 125.

LEAF BASES

5. Cordate. Base shaped
like that of the conven-
tional valentine heart.
Fig. 127.

OBLIQUE   CORDATE
Fig. 126.   Fig. 127.

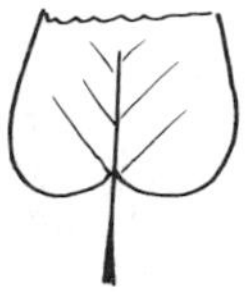

6. Sagittate. Lobed at base,
the lobes pointing backward.
Sometimes used as a term for
general shape. See Fig. 121.
Fig. 128.

7. Hastate. Lobed at base, the
lobes flaring. See Fig. 122.   SAGITTATE   HASTATE
Fig. 129.   Fig. 128. Fig. 129.

APEX.

This refers only to the general area of the tip.

1. Acuminate. Pointed with the two margins somewhat pinched in before joining at the extreme tip. The extreme tip may be broad and short or long and narrow as indicated. Fig. 130.

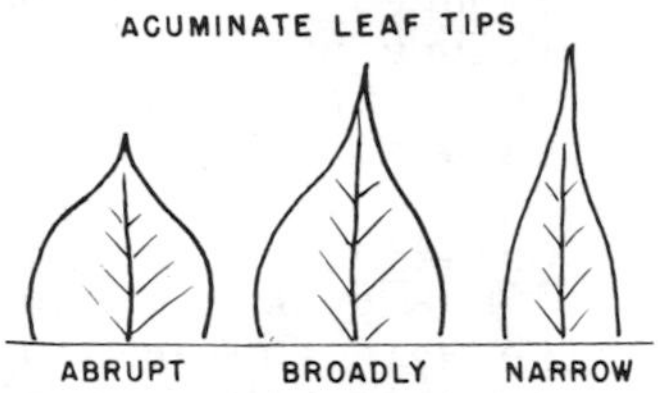

ACUMINATE LEAF TIPS

ABRUPT   BROADLY   NARROW

Fig. 130.

2. Acute. Pointed but the two margins straight until they meet. The leaf may be broadly or narrowly acute. Fig. 131.

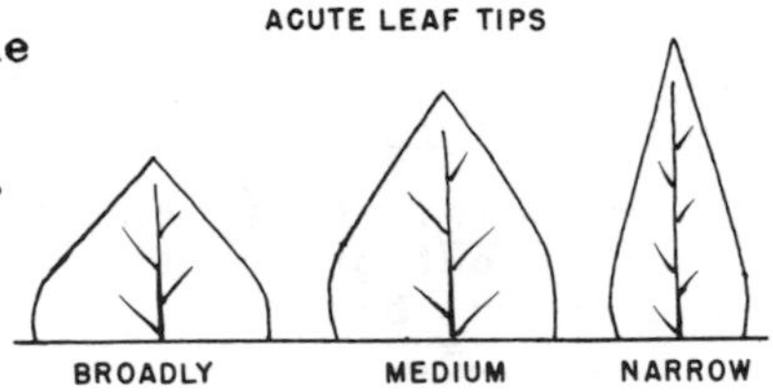

ACUTE LEAF TIPS

BROADLY   MEDIUM   NARROW

Fig. 131.

3. Obtuse. The tip rounded at the extreme end. Fig. 132.

OBTUSE   ROUNDED

4. Rounded. Apex broadly round, really no leaf tip present at all. Some manuals may call this "broadly obtuse". Fig. 133.

Fig. 132 Fig.133

5. Cuspidate. With an abrupt, short sharp firm point. Compare "mucronate". Fig. 134.

CUSPIDATE

6. Mucronate. With an abrupt short tip but this not sharp. Many manuals make no distinction between this and "cuspidate". Fig. 135.

MUCRONATE

Fig. 134. Fig. 135.

7. Aristate. With an awn or stiff bristle at apex. If the awn is small the apex may be called "aristulate". Fig. 136.

ARISTATE   APICULATE

8. Apiculate. Ending in an abrupt slender tip which is not stiff. Fig. 137.

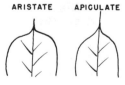

Fig. 136.Fig. 137

52

9. Truncate. The tip appearing cut off by a straight
blade. Fig. 138.

TRUNCATE   EMARGINATE

10. Emarginate. Having a
shallow notch at the broad
apex. See "retuse".
Fig. 139.

Fig. 138.   Fig. 139.

RETUSE

11. Retuse. A shallow notch on a rounded
apex. Many manuals do not make a distinction between this and "emarginate".
Fig. 140.

Fig. 140.

MARGINS

1. Entire. No teeth or
lobes on the margins.
Fig. 141.

2. Repand (undulate).
A gently wavy margin.
Fig. 142.

3. Sinuate. Wavy with
more pronounced undu-
lations. Fig. 143.

ENTIRE   REPAND   SINUATE

Fig. 141.Fig. 142.Fig. 143.

4. Serrate. Toothed with the
teeth directed forward toward the apex of the leaf.
Very small teeth may be called serrulate. Fig. 144.

5. Doubly serrate. With
larger serrate teeth, these
in turn bearing small ser-
rations. Fig. 145.

SERRATE   DOUBLE
           SERRATE

Fig. 144. Fig. 145.

6. Dentate. Toothed but the teeth pointing
outward at right angles to the midline
of the leaf. Such teeth are usually
larger than serrate and some manuals
may loosely call all large teeth
"dentate". Small dentate teeth would be
called "denticulate". Fig. 146.

DENTATE
Fig. 146.

7. Crenate. Toothed with the teeth rounded at their apex. Fig. 147.

CRENATE
Fig. 147.

8. Incised. Leaf cut sharp-ly and usually irregular-ly, with sharp sinuses, deeper than teeth but seldom as deep as one-half way in to the mid-rib or base. Fig. 148.

INCISED MARGINS
Fig. 148.

9. Cleft. Margin cut in about one-half way in to the midrib or base, es-pecially when the sinus is sharp. Fig. 149.

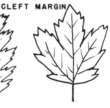

PINNATE   PALMATE
Fig. 149.

10. Lobed. This is often a loosely used term but technically it means cut in not over one-half way in to the midrib or base with the sinuses and tips of the seg-ments rounded. A lobed margin often intergrades with one sinuate. Fig. 150.

LOBED MARGINS

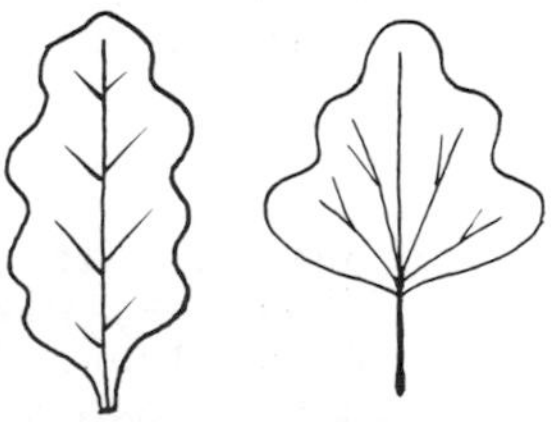

PINNATE   PALMATE
Fig. 150.

11. <u>Parted</u>. The margins are cut in over one-half way to the midrib or base. The sinuses may be sharp or rounded.

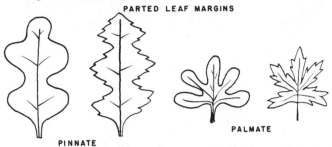

PARTED LEAF MARGINS

PINNATE

PALMATE

Fig. 151.

12. <u>Divided</u>. Cut in to the midrib or to the base. A divided leaf is nearly com-pound but the segments do not form definite units or leaflets. Fig. 152.

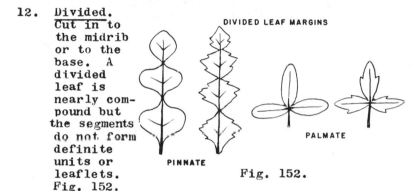

DIVIDED LEAF MARGINS

PINNATE

PALMATE

Fig. 152.

VENATION.

1. <u>Parallel</u>. The veins are small and run more or less parallel, all are about the same size (except sometimes the cen-tral one), and the small connections be-tween them are obscure. Most parallel-veined leaves are long and narrow. Fig. 153.

PARALLEL

Fig.153.

55

2. Netted (reticulated). The veins are large and small, the small ones connecting to each other to form a net. (The minute connections are not shown on the drawing.) Fig. 154.

3. Pinnately veined. With one larger midvein and smaller veins coming off along its length. Fig. 155.

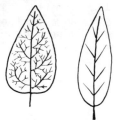

NET   PINNATE

Fig. 154. Fig.155.

4. Palmately veined. With 2 or more large veins arising at or very near the base of the leaf blade. Such leaves are usually rather broad. Fig. 156.

PALMATE

Fig. 156.

56

Chapter IX

TERMS RELATIVE TO SURFACES

The following terms are the ones most commonly applied to the surface of a leaf, usually the under side when no special designation is made since that is the surface that is most apt to be unusual and distinctive. Such terms usually refer either to the lack of hairs or to the particular type of hairs present. Often specific differentiations are based wholly or in part on variations in these surfaces. The terms relative to leaf surfaces are usually considered to be the most difficult of all descriptive terms to master. For example, what is a "long" hair, and how long does it have to be before it ceases to be a "short" hair? Such a question cannot be answered with a concrete measurement.

One way of securing these necessary concepts is to make a practice of checking the surface description as it may be recorded for the plant in the manual, even though such surface characters may not have been needed in the identification. Then compare that description with your specimen. An even better method is to collect several or many outstanding types of different surfaces, try to diagnose each in the following key. Then if at all possible have your examples checked by an expert.

Key to Common Leaf Surfaces
(usually lower)

1. Without hairs or projections

 2. Surface sticky------------------viscid (1.)

 2. Surface not sticky

  3. Waxy, usually glandular
   coat----------------------glaucous (2.)
             (pruinose)

  3. Not waxy   glabrous (3.)

1. With hairs or projections

 4. Hairs on apex or margin only, or these especially noticeable

  5. Hairs at apex only, long, in
   a tuft----------------------comose (4.)

  5. Hairs on margins-----------ciliate (5.)

 4. Hairs or projections scattered on leaf

  6. With short, rough hairs or covered with
   scales

   7. Short rough hairs or rough
    projections------------scabrous (6.)

   7. With scales-------------scurfy (7.)

  6. Hairs short or long but not short and
   rough

   8. Hairs barbed or hooked

    9. Hairs hooked at tip-uncinate (8.)

    9. Hairs barbed

10. Hairs barbed only at
tip------------------------<u>glochidiate</u> (9.)

10. Hairs barbed down sides-----<u>barbellate</u> (10.)

8. Hairs not barbed or hooked

    11. Hairs radially branched or several
arising and spreading from a
common center----------------<u>stellate</u> (11.)

    11. Hairs not branching, not arranged
as above

        12. Hairs curled and interwoven

            13. Very fine and short,
white-------------<u>canescent</u> (12.)

            13. Medium to long

                14. Hairs in scattered
patches--------<u>floccose</u> (13.)

                14. Hairs evenly distributed

                    15. Hairs medium to
short----<u>tomentose</u> (14.)

                    15. Hairs long--<u>lanate</u> (15.)

        12. Hairs fairly straight

            16. Tipped with pinhead-like
glands------------<u>glandular</u> (16.)

            16. No pinhead-like glands

                17. Hairs appressed usually in
one direction and either
short and stiff or long and
silky

                    18. Short, stiff--
<u>strigose</u> (17.)

                    18. Long, silky--
<u>sericeous</u> (18.)

17. Hairs not appressed (or if so not short and stiff or long and silky as above)

   19. Soft short to medium hairs

      20. Very short-<u>puberulent</u> (19.)

      20. Short to medium------<u>pubescent</u> (20.)

   19. Hairs long

      21. Hairs soft

         22. Shaggy hairs----<u>villous</u> (21.)

         22. Hairs not shaggy----<u>pilose</u> (22.)

      21. Hairs moderately to very stiff

         23. Moderately stiff----<u>hirsute</u> (23.)

         23. Very stiff-----<u>hispid</u> (24.)

TYPES OF SURFACES.

    The 24 terms included in the key are explained below and a figure is attempted for most of them. Do not place too much reliance on the drawings since it is almost impossible to give an adequate idea of the types of hairs by a figure. The hairs are drawn in relative size to each other.

1. <u>Viscid</u>. Sticky, as if covered with a thin layer of syrup. The sticky covering may harden in age but such a leaf will have small particles of dust, debris, etc., adhering to its surface.

2. <u>Glaucous</u>. Covered with a waxy, usually whitish covering. This should rub off showing the green of the leaf cells below, but some manuals use the term for any whitish surface. The word

"pruinose" means about the same, often used to designate a conspicuous glaucous covering. An inconspicuous glaucous covering would be "glaucescent".

3. Glabrous. No hairs of any kind present or any other unusual characteristic. A surface that loses its hairs readily and soon becomes glabrous is called "glabrate" or "glabrescent".

4. Comose. With long hairs in a tuft at the apex, the scattered hairs if present at all, much shorter. This term is usually used for seeds. Such a tuft of hairs is called a "coma". Fig. 157.

Fig. 157.

5. Ciliate. Beset with a marginal fringe of hairs. Other hairs may be present but are much less conspicuous. When the hairs are coarse and crowded the condition may be called "fimbriate". Fig. 158.

Fig. 158.

6. Scabrous. Rough and rasp-like when gently rubbed with the finger tip. This roughness may be caused by short, stiff hairs or short sharp projections. Fig. 159.

Fig. 159.

7. Scurfy. Surface covered with small, often overlapping scale-like particles. These are usually definite enough to be seen with a hand lens. Fig. 160.

Fig. 160.

8. Uncinate. Stiff hairs or bristles hooked at the apex, usually used for the surfaces of fruits instead of for leaves. Fig. 161.

UNCINATE

GLOCHIDIATE

9. Glochidiate. Stiff hairs or bristles barbed at the apex. Fig. 162.

Fig. 161.   Fig. 162.

10. Barbellate. Stiff hairs or bristles barbed down the sides (usually at apex too). Fig. 163.

BARBELLATE

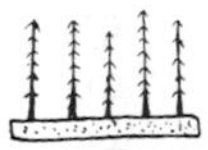

Fig. 163.

11. Stellate. Star-like or star-shaped with slender segments or hairs radiating out from a common center. Fig. 164.

STELLATE HAIRS
Fig. 164.

12. Canescent. The surface more or less densely covered with white or gray short hairs, giving that color to the surface. The term is sometimes loosely used to mean any gray or white surface. Fig. 165.

CANESCENT

Fig. 165.

FLOCCOSE

13. Floccose. Surface with medium to long interwoven hairs, these occurring in scattered patches. Fig. 166.

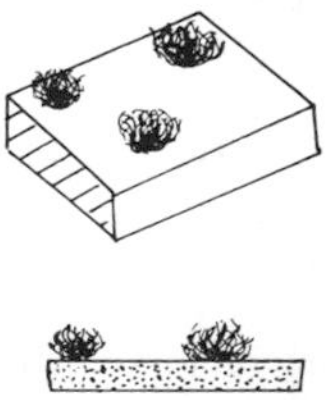

Fig. 166.

14. Tomentose. Covered with interwoven short to medium length hairs, this covering usually dense enough to conceal the true leaf surface. Fig. 167.

TOMENTOSE

LANATE

15. Lanate. With interwoven long hairs. Fig. 168.

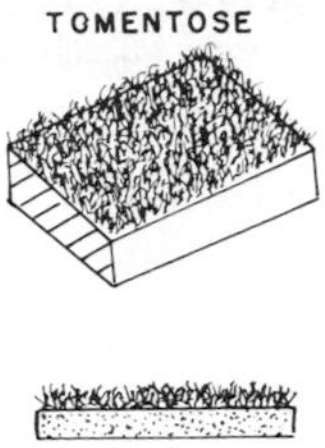

Fig. 167. 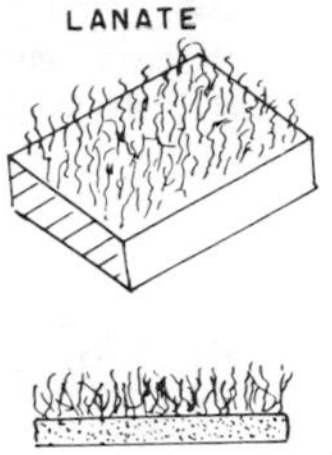   Fig. 168.

16. Glandular. Hairs are called glandular when they are tipped with pinhead-like enlargements, these sometimes strikingly colored. Fig. 169.

GLANDULAR HAIRS
Fig. 169.

STRIGOSE

17. Strigose. With appressed rather short and stiff hairs. When the hairs are very short the surface would be called "strigillose". Fig. 170.

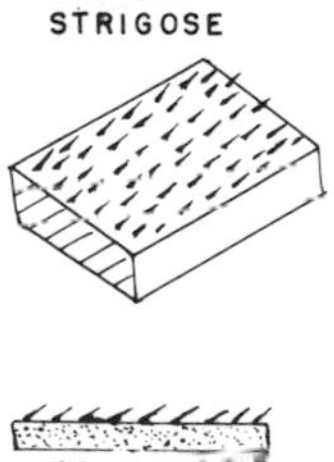

Fig. 170.

18. Sericeous. Covered with long straight soft, appressed hairs giving a silky effect. The hairs are more numerous than indicated on the drawing. Fig. 171.

SERICEOUS
Fig. 171.

PUBERULENT

19. Puberulent. With very short hairs. Fig. 172.

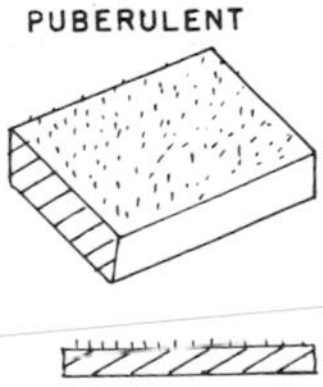

Fig. 172.

20. **Pubescent.** With short to medium length hairs. This term is sometimes used to mean with hairs of any type. Fig. 173.

PUBESCENT
Fig. 173.

21. **Villous.** With long soft, somewhat wavy hairs. Fig. 174.

VILLOUS

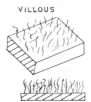

Fig. 174.

22. **Pilose.** With long, soft, nearly straight hairs. Many manuals do not differentiate this term from "villous". Fig. 175.

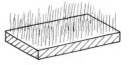

PILOSE
Fig. 175.

23. **Hirsute.** With long moderately stiff hairs. A less pronounced hirsute condition may be called "hirsutulous" (or hirsutulose). Fig. 176.

HIRSUTE

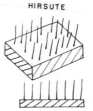

Fig. 176.

24. **Hispid.** With long very stiff hairs, these usually sharp and stiff enough to penetrate the skin of the hands. A less pronounced hispid condition may be called "hispidulous". Fig. 177.

HISPID

Fig. 177.

64

Chapter X

GENERAL TERMS

This chapter explains terms that are in common
use but did not seem to fit in any other place.

1. Tendril. A slender modified stem or leaf, commonly coiling at the apex and
serving as an organ of support. Fig. 178.

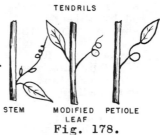
TENDRILS

STEM   MODIFIED   PETIOLE
LEAF
Fig. 178.

2. Aquatic plant. A plant that must live partly or
entirely in water for at least part of its life
cycle. A true aquatic plant often has a weak
flaccid stem and dissected leaves.

3. Terrestrial. A plant growing in the air with its
basal parts in wet or dry soil.

4. Fern-like. A plant with filmy-dissected leaves
on the general order of those of a fern plant.
See Fig. 102.

5. Rush-like. A grass-like
plant with very small inconspicuous flowers and typical
long linear grass-like leaves.
The drawing to the right shows
a flower split longitudinally
and only one-half indicated.
Fig. 179.

RUSH
Fig. 179.

6. Grass-like. A grass-like plant with long linear grass-like leaves and very inconspicuous flowers. The round drawing to the right shows a grass stem (culm) in cross-section surrounded by a leaf sheath. Fig. 180.

7. Moss-like. Resembling the common moss plant, with rather short and slender stems crowded with small thin leaves. The drawing shows 2 spore-bearing capsules of a moss plant. Fig. 181.

8. Heath-like. Resembling a heath, with thick, small, entire-margined leaves, these often partly rolled. Fig. 182.

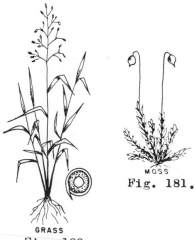

GRASS

Fig. 180.

MOSS

Fig. 181.

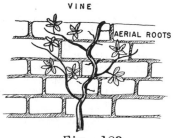

HEATH LIKE

SECTION OF LEAF

Fig. 182.

9. Vine. A plant climbing or scrambling on some other support. Such a plant may support itself by tendrils, or aerial roots as in the figure. Fig. 183.

VINE

AERIAL ROOTS

Fig. 183.

66

10. Tree. A woody plant of considerable stature at maturity,
with one or few main trunks.
This term is often loosely used
and although hard to define is
a fairly well understood concept. Fig. 184.

TREE

Fig. 184.

11. Shrub. A woody plant smaller at
maturity than a tree and usually with
several basal stems. Fig. 185.

SHRUB

Fig. 185.

12. Parasite. A plant growing upon and obtaining
nourishment from another organism, usually lacking green chlorophyll.

13. Saprophyte. A plant that obtains its food from
dead organic material instead of manufacturing
it through the more usual process of photosynthesis. Such a plant is commonly light green
in color or may be lacking green chlorophyll
entirely.

14. Family. A group of related genera.

15. Genus. A group of related species.

16. Species. This has been variously defined but
it is a term for all the individuals of one
kind - from a practical standpoint to students -
those plants that key to and match the same
specific description as outlined in the manuals.

17. Subspecies. One of the variants of a species,
not distinct enough to warrant a separate
specific name, but different enough to be given
a designation.

18. Variety. Used by many authors with the same
meaning as "subspecies". Used by others with a-
bout the same meaning as "forma". The botanical
"variety" may be much different from the horticultural one.

19. Forma. A very minor variant, such as a white-
     flowered plant among a population of blue-
     flowered ones. The botanists who use the term
     "subspecies" for a major variant may use the
     term "variety" for a minor one. This sounds
     rather confusing, but the beginning student
     merely has to follow the usage of the manual he
     is employing.

TEST FOR GENERAL UNDERSTANDING OF PLANTS.

     The following outline will give you a chance to
check up on your ability to properly diagnose a
plant, the first requisite in identifying. Try to
answer the 25 questions without consulting a glossary, then if at all possible have your answers
checked by an expert. A high score indicates that
you have the essential terms in mind so that identification should be reasonably rapid. Several extra
pages of this test are included so you can check
yourself on more than one plant, or the outline can
be used as a formal test in a class.

Write the word that answers the question in the blank space before the number.

Words underlined are to be used in these answers.

Be sure your specimen is not abnormal or badly shattered. For number of parts give the average of several determinations.

_____ 1. Is the plant annual or perennial?

_____ 2. Are rhizomes present or absent?

_____ 3. Name type of inflorescence.

_____ 4. How many sepals?

_____ 5. How many petals?

_____ 6. How many stamens?

_____ 7. How many pistils?

_____ 8. How many carpels to each pistil?

_____ 9. How many locules to each ovary?

_____ 10. Are ovules one, two, several or many to each cell?

_____ 11. Is placentation axile, parietal, basal or free central?

_____ 12. Are stamens opposite or alternate to petals? (or both or neither?)

_____ 13. How many styles to each ovary?

_____ 14. How many stigmas or stigma lobes to each ovary?

_____ 15. Is the flower regular or irregular?

_____ 16. Are the petals separate or united?

_____ 17. Is the flower epigynous, perigynous or hypogynous?

_____ 18. Is the ovary superior or inferior?

_____ 19. Is the stem leafy or scapose?

_____ 20. Are leaves opposite, alternate,
                      whorled, radical or basal?

_____ 21. Are bracts present? (yes or no).

_____ 22. Are the leaves simple or compound?
                      (If compound what special type?)

_____ 23. What term best describes the leaf
                      shape (or leaflet on a compound
                      leaf)?

_____ 24. What term best describes the leaf
                      margin (or leaflet)?

_____ 25. What term best describes the leaf
                      surface (usually lower side)?

Write the word that answers the question in the blank space before the number.

Words underlined are to be used in these answers.

Be sure your specimen is not abnormal or badly shattered. For number of parts give the average of several determinations.

_____ 1. Is the plant annual or perennial?

_____ 2. Are rhizomes present or absent?

_____ 3. Name type of inflorescence.

_____ 4. How many sepals?

_____ 5. How many petals?

_____ 6. How many stamens?

_____ 7. How many pistils?

_____ 8. How many carpels to each pistil?

_____ 9. How many locules to each ovary?

_____ 10. Are ovules one, two, several or many to each cell?

_____ 11. Is placentation axile, parietal, basal or free central?

_____ 12. Are stamens opposite or alternate to petals? (or both or neither?)

_____ 13. How many styles to each ovary?

_____ 14. How many stigmas or stigma lobes to each ovary?

_____ 15. Is the flower regular or irregular?

_____ 16. Are the petals separate or united?

_____ 17. Is the flower epigynous, perigynous or hypogynous?

69b

_____ 18. Is the ovary superior or inferior?

_____ 19. Is the stem leafy or scapose?

_____ 20. Are leaves opposite, alternate, whorled, radical or basal?

_____ 21. Are bracts present? (yes or no).

_____ 22. Are the leaves simple or compound? (If compound what special type?)

_____ 23. What term best describes the leaf shape (or leaflet on a compound leaf)?

_____ 24. What term best describes the leaf margin (or leaflet)?

_____ 25. What term best describes the leaf surface (usually lower side)?

Write the word that answers the question in the blank space before the number.

Words <u>underlined</u> are to be used in these answers.

Be sure your specimen is not abnormal or badly shattered. For number of parts give the average of several determinations.

_____ 1. Is the plant <u>annual</u> or <u>perennial</u>?

_____ 2. Are rhizomes <u>present</u> or <u>absent</u>?

_____ 3. Name type of inflorescence.

_____ 4. How many sepals?

_____ 5. How many petals?

_____ 6. How many stamens?

_____ 7. How many pistils?

_____ 8. How many carpels to each pistil?

_____ 9. How many locules to each ovary?

_____ 10. Are ovules <u>one</u>, <u>two</u>, <u>several</u> or <u>many</u> to each cell?

_____ 11. Is placentation <u>axile</u>, <u>parietal</u>, <u>basal</u> or <u>free central</u>?

_____ 12. Are stamens <u>opposite</u> or <u>alternate</u> to petals? (or <u>both</u> or <u>neither</u>?)

_____ 13. How many styles to each ovary?

_____ 14. How many stigmas or stigma lobes to each ovary?

_____ 15. Is the flower <u>regular</u> or <u>irregular</u>?

_____ 16. Are the petals <u>separate</u> or <u>united</u>?

_____ 17. Is the flower <u>epigynous</u>, <u>perigynous</u> or <u>hypogynous</u>?

_____ 18. Is the ovary <u>superior</u> or <u>inferior</u>?

_____ 19. Is the stem <u>leafy</u> or <u>scapose</u>?

_____ 20. Are leaves <u>opposite</u>, <u>alternate</u>, <u>whorled</u>, <u>radical</u> or <u>basal</u>?

_____ 21. Are bracts present? (<u>yes</u> or <u>no</u>).

_____ 22. Are the leaves <u>simple</u> or <u>compound</u>? (If compound what special type?)

_____ 23. What term best describes the leaf shape (or leaflet on a compound leaf)?

_____ 24. What term best describes the leaf margin (or leaflet)?

_____ 25. What term best describes the leaf surface (usually lower side)?

Write the word that answers the question in the blank space before the number.

Words underlined are to be used in these answers.

Be sure your specimen is not abnormal or badly shattered. For number of parts give the average of several determinations.

_____	1.	Is the plant annual or perennial?
_____	2.	Are rhizomes present or absent?
_____	3.	Name type of inflorescence.
_____	4.	How many sepals?
_____	5.	How many petals?
_____	6.	How many stamens?
_____	7.	How many pistils?
_____	8.	How many carpels to each pistil?
_____	9.	How many locules to each ovary?
_____	10.	Are ovules one, two, several or many to each cell?
_____	11.	Is placentation axile, parietal, basal or free central?
_____	12.	Are stamens opposite or alternate to petals? (or both or neither?)
_____	13.	How many styles to each ovary?
_____	14.	How many stigmas or stigma lobes to each ovary?
_____	15.	Is the flower regular or irregular?
_____	16.	Are the petals separate or united?
_____	17.	Is the flower epigynous, perigynous or hypogynous?

69d

_____ 18. Is the ovary <u>superior</u> or <u>inferior</u>?

_____ 19. Is the stem <u>leafy</u> or <u>scapose</u>?

_____ 20. Are leaves <u>opposite</u>, <u>alternate</u>, <u>whorled</u>, <u>radical</u> or <u>basal</u>?

_____ 21. Are bracts present? (<u>yes</u> or <u>no</u>).

_____ 22. Are the leaves <u>simple</u> or <u>compound</u>? (If compound what <u>special type</u>?)

_____ 23. What term best describes the leaf shape (or leaflet on a compound leaf)?

_____ 24. What term best describes the leaf margin (or leaflet)?

_____ 25. What term best describes the leaf surface (usually lower side)?

Chapter XI

FRUITS AND SEEDS

DEFINITIONS.

Fruit.

The fruit is the ripened ovary and any other structure that is closely associated with it.

Seed.

The seed is the matured ovule, containing the small plant (embryo) with a food supply to initiate its development.

Misconceptions.

Many actual fruits are known as "seeds" to the gardner and farmer. The kernel of corn, wheat, or oats, the so-called "seed" of the sunflower, carrot or parsnip is in reality a fruit containing one or two seeds. To many people a "fruit" implies a fleshy structure but this is not necessarily so.

USE OF FRUITS IN IDENTIFICATION.

Differences in fruit types may be used to construct categories in the generic or specific keys. This occurs in the mustard (Cruciferae) and parsley (Umbelliferae) families, as well as in others such as the rose (Rosaceae), legume (Leguminosae) and buttercup (Ranunculaceae) families.

This not only necessitates a clear understanding of fruit types and terms but often creates an additional problem. Flower characters are always used, at least in identifying the plant to the family but flowers and the necessary fruit may not occur together. The thing to do in such a case is to collect a plant in flower, note its floral characters, even saving a specimen if at all possible, then collect a plant later on in fruiting condition. Often an ideal situation occurs and a plant may bear both flowers and fruit at the same time. More

71

commonly still, when several individual plants are examined, some may be in flower and others in fruit. Sometimes the old fruit of the preceding year may remain on the plant or on the ground beneath the plant to help out in this respect.

TERMS NEEDED TO UNDERSTAND THE FRUIT KEY.

Before attempting to diagnose a fruit using the key following this unit it will be necessary to understand a few terms.

1. Pericarp. The ripened wall of the matured ovary in the fruit is called a pericarp. Sometimes three layers can be distinguished, the outer exocarp, the middle mesocarp and the inner endocarp. (See Fig. 188 under "drupe".)

2. Fleshy. This means succulent and watery at maturity like an apple, cherry, raspberry or tomato.

3. Dry. Dry at maturity. For example a bean pod is fleshy and edible when young but becomes dry upon ripening.

4. Dehiscent. A fruit that opens naturally to release the enclosed seed or seeds.

5. Suture. A suture is the line of dehiscence. (See Fig. 186.)

6. Septum. A partition between the cells of an ovary or fruit. (See Fig. 186.)

7. Valve. One of the segments of a dehiscent fruit after opening. The right-hand drawing shows a cross-section of the fruit before the valves have separated widely. Fig. 186.

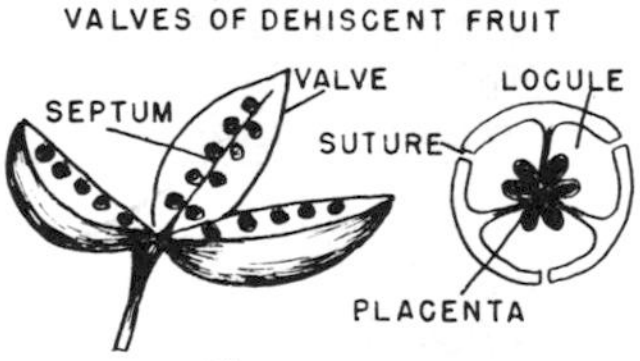

VALVES OF DEHISCENT FRUIT

SEPTUM VALVE LOGULE SUTURE PLACENTA

Fig. 186.

8. Indehiscent. A fruit that does not open to release the seed or seeds. Fleshy fruits are practically always indehiscent as are most dry one-seeded fruits. The seed eventually may germinate and force its way through the walls of the fruit unless these have already decayed away.

72

9. Locule (cell). One of the compartments of an
    ovary or fruit. (See Fig. 186 under "valve".)

10. Carpel. One of the individ-
    ual parts of a compound
    ovary, theoretically that
    part formed from one sporo-
    phyll in its evolutionary de-
    velopment. The rule is to
    count the number of locules
    (cells), placentae, styles
    and stigma lobes. The high-
    est number will be the num-
    ber of carpels. This whole situation is dis-
    cussed and figured at the end of Chapter IV.
    In the 3 figures above, the center one would
    have 1 carpel if the ovary had but one cell and
    one placenta. The other two figures show
    ovaries or fruits in cross-section, with three
    carpels indicated for each. Fig. 187.

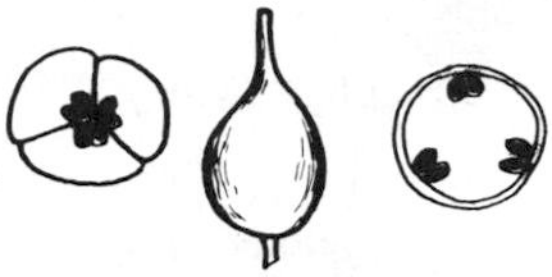

CARPELS

Fig. 187.

Key to the Common Fruits

1. Fruit fleshy

    2. Pistil one, simple, one-seeded,
    endocarp stony------------Drupe (Plum) (1.)

    2. Pistils either more than one, or if one with
    more than one carpel and usually many seeded,
    endocarp not stony

        3. Pistils more than one, from the same
        flower or from more than one flower

            4. Pistils of one flower forming indi-
            vidual fruit

                5. Receptacle very fleshy, pistils
                achene-like,
                dry---Accessory (Strawberry) (2.)

                5. Receptacle not very fleshy,
                pistils drupe-like,
                fleshy-Aggregate (Raspberry) (3.)

            4. Pistils from more than one flower
            forming one individual fruit

                6. Bulk of fruit from a hypanthium,
                which encloses many
                pistils-------Syconium (Fig) (4.)

                6. Bulk of fruit from many fleshy,
                  superior pistils densely
                clustered-Multiple (Mulberry)(5.)

        3. Pistil one to a fruit, compound

            7. Ovary superior, receptacle not form-
            ing part of fruit

                8. Covering of fruit thin, not
                leathery------Berry (Tomato) (6.)

                8. Covering of fruit thick and
                leathery-Hesperidium (Orange)(7.)

7. Ovary inferior, receptacle (or calyx tube)
    forming part of fruit

    9. Receptacle forming only a tough, hard,
        outer rind--------Pepo (Watermelon) (8.)

    9. Receptacle fleshy, thick, forming the
        bulk of the fruit------Pome (Apple) (9.)

1. Fruit dry at maturity, not fleshy

    10. Indehiscent, the seeds not falling out of
         fruit, usually one-seeded (2-seeded in
         (Schizocarps and some Samaras)

         11. Fruit of 2 or more carpels that sepa-
              rate at maturity leaving the common
              axis between them--
                        Schizocarp (Carrot) (10.)

         11. Only one carpel, or if two (as in some
              Samaras) not leaving an axis between
              when they separate

              12. Fruit winged-
                        Samara (Maple, Ash) (11.)

              12. Fruit not winged

                   13. Wall tough and hard-
                        Nut (Acorn, Walnut) (12.)
                        (A small nut-like fruit is a
                        nutlet.)

                   13. Wall not especially hard and
                        tough

                        14. Seed attached to ovary
                             wall at only one point-
                             Achene (Sunflower)(13.)

                        14. Seed attached to ovary
                             wall at all points-
                             Caryopsis (Corn,
                                        Wheat) (14.)

    10. Dehiscent, the seeds commonly many

15. Only one line of dehiscence, ovary of one
     carpel----------------<u>Follicle</u> (Milkweed) (15.)

15. Two or more lines of dehiscence, ovary of one
     or more than one carpel

     16. Fruit one-celled, one carpel present

          17. Pod constricted between the seeds,
               tending to break into one-seeded
               segments--<u>Loment</u> (Beggar's Lice)(16.)

          17. Pod not especially constricted, not
               breaking up---<u>Legume</u> (Pea, Bean)(17.)

     16. Fruit more than one-celled (partition thin
          and sometimes hard to see in a silique and
          silicle), or if one-celled, with 2 or more
          carpels present

          18. The two carpels pulling away leaving
               a thin central septum

               19. Fruit short and broad
                         <u>Silicle</u> (Pepper grass) (18.)

               19. Fruit long and narrow
                         <u>Silique</u> (Mustard) (19.)

          18. Carpels as they pull apart leaving no
               partition in the center (or opening
               by pores or lids at apex), often over
               two carpels present-
                         <u>Capsule</u> (Lily) (20.)

               There are 4 types of capsules:-
               Opening by pores-
                         <u>Poricidal</u> (Poppy) (20A.)

               Opening along septa
                         <u>Septicidal</u> (Yucca) (20B.)

               Opening along middle of locule
                         <u>Loculicidal</u> (Iris) (20C.)

               Opening by a lid, along a circular
               horizontal line--Circumscissile or a
                    pyxis (Purslane, Plantain) (20D.)

76

DEFINITIONS AND DRAWINGS OF THE FRUITS IN THE KEY.

1. Drupe. A fleshy indehiscent fruit, one-seeded, with the endocarp stony. Fig. 188.

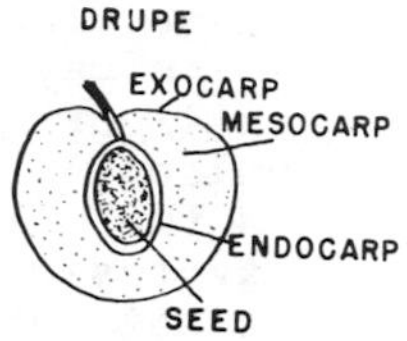

DRUPE

EXOCARP
MESOCARP
ENDOCARP
SEED

Fig. 188.

2. Accessory. A fleshy fruit like a strawberry, made up of a succulent receptacle covered with several to many pistils, each forming a dry achene-like fruit. Sometimes not distinguished from aggregate. Fig. 189.

ACCESSORY FRUIT

FLESHY RECEPTACLE
ACHENES

Fig. 189.

3. Aggregate. A fruit with the receptacle not especially fleshy, with several to many pistils, these each becoming fleshy and drupe-like. The blackberry and raspberry are examples. In the lefthand drawing the cluster of drupes has been removed leaving the naked receptacle, as occurs in the raspberry. Fig. 190.

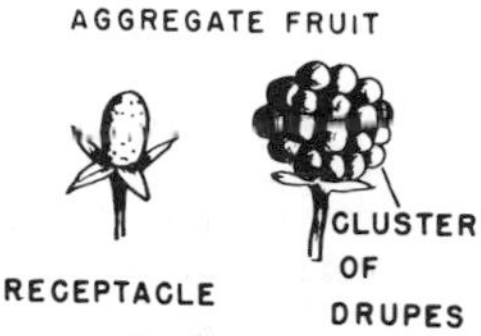

AGGREGATE FRUIT

CLUSTER OF DRUPES
RECEPTACLE

Fig. 190.

4. Syconium. A fruit made up of a fleshy hollow receptacle bearing inside many small separate flowers, each of which may produce a seed-like nutlet. A Fig is a good example. In the drawing the fruit is shown in longitudinal section. Fig. 191.

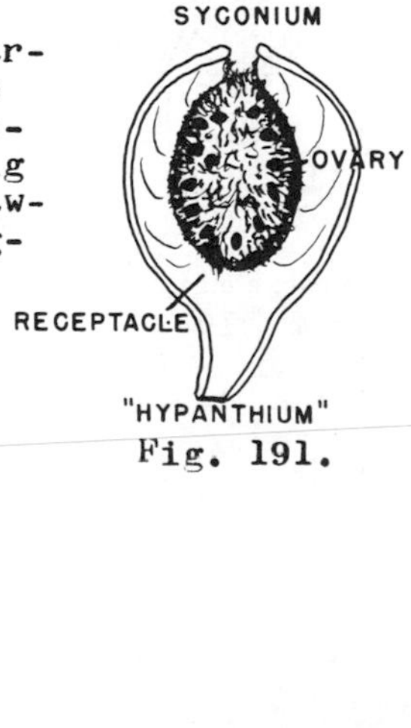

SYCONIUM

OVARY
RECEPTACLE
"HYPANTHIUM"

Fig. 191.

77

5. <u>Multiple</u>. A fleshy fruit formed from several to many separate flowers. These flowers have superior ovaries which may become fleshy but other parts of the unit may also be succulent. The classic example is borne on the mulberry plant. Such a fruit may resemble an aggregate fruit but is not formed from one flower. Fig. 192.

MULTIPLE FRUIT

Fig. 192.

6. <u>Berry</u>. A fleshy fruit formed from one compound ovary containing few to many seeds. This fruit appears in the key as formed from a superior ovary, however, the term is often loosely used to include pulpy fruits formed from an inferior ovary but not resembling a pepo or pome. Fig. 193.

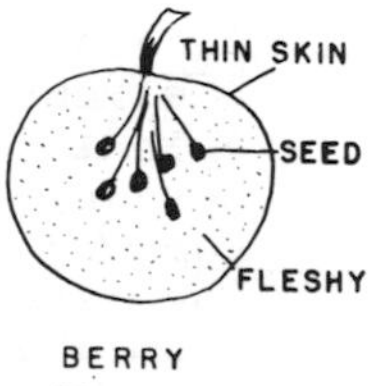

THIN SKIN

SEED

FLESHY

BERRY

Fig. 193.

7. <u>Hesperidium</u>. This is a berry-like fruit with a thick leathery covering. An orange is a good example. Fig. 194.

8. <u>Pepo</u>. A fleshy fruit formed from a compound inferior ovary, the outer wall becoming rather hard and tough. Watermelon and cucumber have this type of fruit. Fig. 195.

9. <u>Pome</u>. A fleshy fruit formed from an inferior compound ovary, the receptacle (or calyx tube) fleshy and thick. The apple is a pome. Fig. 196.

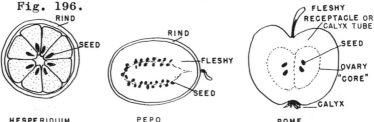

RIND

SEED

HESPERIDIUM
Fig. 194.

RIND

FLESHY

SEED

PEPO
Fig. 195.

FLESHY RECEPTACLE OR CALYX TUBE

SEED

OVARY "CORE"

CALYX

POME
Fig. 196.

10. Schizocarp. A dry indehiscent fruit made up of
2 or more 1-seeded carpels
that separate at maturity
leaving a common axis be-
tween (the carpophore).
Sometimes each segment is
called a "mericarp". The
drawing to the left shows a
cross-section of such a
fruit. Some manuals may
call this fruit a cremo-
carp. Fig. 197.

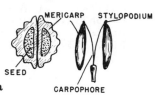

SCHIZOCARP

Fig. 197.

11. Samara. A dry indehiscent
winged fruit like those on
a maple (double samara) or
ash (single). Fig. 198.

Fig. 198.

12. Nut. A dry, indehiscent one-seeded fruit with
a hard coat. Often rather loosely used.

13. Achene. A dry indehiscent one-
seeded fruit, the seed connected
to the pericarp at only one point.
The sunflower has achenes. In the
figure the seed is shown as if
shrunken away from the pericarp.
Fig. 199.

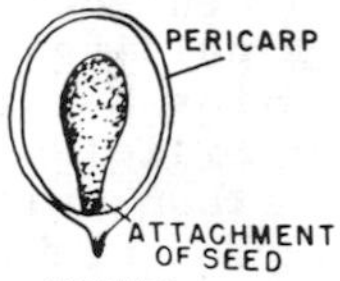

14. Caryopsis (grain). A dry
indehiscent one-seeded
fruit, the seed connected
to the pericarp at all
points. The corn kernel
is a caryopsis. Fig. 200.

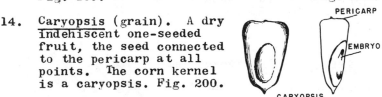

ACHENE

Fig. 199.

CARYOPSIS

Fig. 200.

15. **Follicle.** A dry one-celled, one-carpellate fruit splitting down one side only, as in the milkweed. Fig. 201.

FOLLICLE
Fig. 201.

16. **Loment.** A dry one-celled, one-carpellate fruit constricted between the seeds. Otherwise like the more common legume. Fig. 202.

Fig. 202.

17. **Legume.** A dry one-celled, one-carpellate fruit splitting down two sides. Often called a "pod", a loosely used term. Fig. 203.

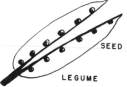

Fig. 203.

18. **Silicle.** A dry two-celled dehiscent fruit, each half pulling away at maturity leaving a thin central septum. A silicle is usually not more than twice as long as wide. The righthand drawing shows the 2 valves pulled away from the septum and pushed to the sides. Fig. 204.

SILICLE
Fig. 204.

19. **Silique.** A dry two-celled dehiscent fruit each half pulling away at maturity leaving a thin central septum. The length is more than twice the width. Fig. 205.

SILIQUE
Fig. 205.

20. Capsule. A dry dehiscent fruit made up of more than one carpel. It may be one-celled with one line of dehiscence but the placentae would be more than one. This is a very common type of fruit.

   A. Poricidal capsule. One that opens by means of pores, as in a poppy. Fig. 206.

   B. Septicidal capsule. One that opens along the septa by splitting it. Fig. 207.

   C. Loculicidal capsule. One that opens along the middle of the locule. Fig. 208.

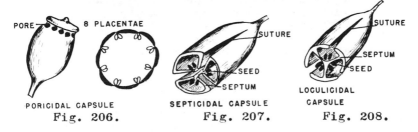

PORICIDAL CAPSULE
Fig. 206.

SEPTICIDAL CAPSULE
Fig. 207.

LOCULICIDAL CAPSULE
Fig. 208.

   D. Circumscissile capsule (pyxis). One that opens by a lid along a circular horizontal line. Fig. 209.

CIRCUMSCISSILE CAPSULE

Fig. 209.

SEEDS.

   Mature seeds are usually not yet present on a plant that bears the flowers necessary for identification. However, in some genera like Mentzelia and Epilobium seed characters may actually be used as categories in the key. In such cases seeds may be obtained from more mature individuals or even from fruits of the preceding year. The various Seed Testing Laboratories have developed a technique whereby they can identify the seeds and small fruits of common weeds when they come in as a contaminate in crop seeds, but here the actual possibilities are limited of course.

VARIATIONS OF SEEDS.

Seeds vary in different ways, the commonest ones listed below.

1. Size. The coconut has a very large seed, the orchid a very small one.

2. Hairs. Some seeds bear hairs such as in Epilobium (fireweed) and Asclepias (milkweed), these function in aiding the distribution of these objects by the wind.

3. Wings. Some seeds as well as some fruits have wings, like those borne by some species of Mentzelia (stickleaf); these may be used in classification.

4. Shape. The typical shape is round or oval but seeds may vary widely in this respect.

5. Color. Seeds may vary strikingly in color but sometimes the difference may be so subtle that it can be perceived only by trained eyes like those of an expert seed analyst. An example of a conspicuous color is found in a species of Sophora (coral bean) which has a bright scarlet seed.

6. Surface markings. Seeds may have very elaborate and striking designs and surface sculpturings, these often taking the form of raised or indented tracery.

7. Hilum and raphe. The scar where the seed broke away from the fruit (hilum) and the ridge that appears adjacent to it (raphe) often vary in shape, prominence, position, etc. Fig. 210.

RAPHE
HILUM
MICROPYLE

TYPICAL SEED

Fig. 210.

8. Embryo. The position, size, shape and number of the cotyledons is sometimes used in families like the Chenopodiaceae (Goosefoot family). This means that mature seeds and fruit are necessary in order to secure a positive check on this character, which means a rather close study under a dissecting microscope or good hand lens.

Chapter XII

USE OF KEYS IN PLANT IDENTIFICATION

WHY KEYS ARE NECESSARY.

Keys provide a convenient short cut method of de-
termining plants by outlining and grouping related
types. There is a particular "knack" in using keys,
gained partly by certain native ability in weighing
evidence in order to arrive at a correct decision,
but obtained mostly by constant practice and experience. If the student has in mind a good concept as
to the meaning of the common descriptive terms and a
correct understanding of the characters of the plant
under consideration, then identifying it through the
key should not be so difficult.

TYPES OF KEYS.

1. Synoptical. This key runs through the descrip-
    tions as headings. Often more than one choice
    is presented and usually more than one species
    (in specific key) is listed under the last head-
    ing. This involves reading over several specific
    descriptions as the final step. Only the older
    manuals use this type of key, consequently no ex-
    ample is given here.

2. Bracket. In this key the two choices always
    stand together. An example would be:

1. Flowers red---------------------------------- 2

1. Flowers blue--------------------------------- 5

    2. Leaves simple---------------------------- 3

    2. Leaves compound------------------------- 4

3. Petals 4--------------------------Species no. 1

3. Petals 5--------------------------Species no. 2

    4. Leaflets 5--------------------Species no. 3

    4. Leaflets 9-11----------------Species no. 4

5.   Flowers sessile--------------------Species no. 5

5.   Flowers pedicelled----------------------------6

    6.   Inflorescence a raceme---------Species no. 6

    6.   Inflorescence a panicle--------Species no. 7

        Some authors do not even indent every other pair of choices. In any case the bracket key saves space and is easier to set up for printing. However, it does not outline the group in as definite a manner as the Indented Key and is more difficult to use if it is necessary to "try" both categories (See Hints in Using Keys, number 3).

3.   Indented Key. Here the group is outlined and better organized as each new pair of choices is set off by an indentation. In the example given the pairs have a like number to aid in locating the contrasting choice. This is particularly useful in a long key where the other member of the pair may be several pages distant. When no numbers are used you find the opposite choice by similarity in indentation and also by comparing the context which should be in contrast in the two categories. The key given below is for the same plants that were treated in the Bracket Key.

1.   Flowers red

    2.   Leaves simple

        3.   Petals 4-------------------Species no. 1

        3.   Petals 5-------------------Species no. 2

    2.   Leaves compound

        4.   Leaflets 5----------------Species no. 3

        4.   Leaflets 9-11--------------Species no. 4

1.   Flowers blue

    5.   Flowers sessile----------------Species no. 5

    5.   Flowers pedicelled

        6.   Inflorescence a raceme-----Species no. 6

        6.   Inflorescence a panicle----Species no. 7

    Notice that all the red flowers fall together
making a more logical outline of the group. The
majority of the modern manuals use this type of key.
It does waste some space to the left of the page
and is a typist's nightmare but most botanists prefer to use such a key over the Bracket type.

DIFFICULTIES IN USING KEYS.

    Like the human beings that create them, botanical
keys are not perfect. Listed below are some of the
difficulties you can expect to encounter in using
keys. Do not be too ready to find fault with the
author of your treatment, at least until you are certain you yourself have not made a blunder. An excellent way to gain sympathy for the creator of your
keys is to try your own hand at making one. Some
suggestions for handling some of these difficulties
will be given later on in this chapter.

1.   The key may use characters not present on your
      specimen. For example the generic key to the
      family Ranunculaceae (Buttercup Family) is usual-
      ly based on the type of fruit, but floral char-
      acters are necessary to key the plant to the
      family. If your plant does not have both flowers
      and fruit you have a problem.

2.   The key is set up for the average plant. Your
      specimen may be abnormal in some way. The remedy
      is to select one or more average plants and avoid
      the unusual or freakish specimens.

3.   In some keys the author may ring in more than 2
      choices. This is especially disconcerting if the
      third choice happens to fall on a different page.
      However, few if any of the recently printed man-
      uals have this fault.

4.   The exact meaning of some terms may vary with the
      different manuals used. Certain terms like
      caespitose, canescent, elliptic, membranous,
      decumbent and pubescent are loosely used by some
      botanists. If you use one manual only, this
      problem should not arise.

5. The meanings of some terms vary somewhat when used for different groups. "Plants tall" may mean a few centimeters when used with Stellaria (Chickweed) or it may mean several meters tall when used with Betula (Birch tree). Similarly the size of a "large flowered" buttercup would give you a "small flowered" rose. The remedy of course would be for your manual to use concrete measurements with the understanding that unusual specimens may fall above or below the figure given.

6. The characters given in the first category of the pair may not be all contrasted in the second. This seems to be a very common fault in key making where secondary characters are stated in one place and ignored in the other. For example, you may read "Flowers white; plants annual" as contrasted to "Flowers yellow". Very often the duration habit of the yellow flowered plants can be puzzled out by reading further in the key.

7. Keys are in fine print and it is easy to overlook a line entirely and miss an important step. The remedy is to take your time in using a key.

8. The key may be actually ambiguous or faulty in places due to an out-and-out mistake of the author. This is unfortunate because as a student you have to trust your key. A teacher in the laboratory can help you over such places. If you are on your own all you can do is to check your plant again, perhaps try other parts of the key, then if you always come back to the same place you might suspect an error in the treatment. For example, if you always arrive at 2 choices, "Flowers red" as opposed to "Flowers white" with a yellow flowered plant, it may be that the writer of the key inadvertently left off the "or yellow" and the last choice should have read, "Flowers white or yellow". You can check on this by trial.

    Sometimes the "exception" is not properly provided for, especially in a manual treating large numbers of plants. For example, in a blue-flowered genus one species may have white flowers. This may be overlooked and the generic key may put the genus under "flowers blue" only.

86

The particular "knack" in using keys in a large part is in being able to sense when the key is faulty or misleading. This is easier to do after you have had considerable experience following one manual.

9. The plant you are trying to identify may not be included in the key. You may have a weedy species that has come in since the book was written and may even have become locally abundant. Or your plant may be a rare one whose exact limits were not understood at the time the manual was written. When you come to suspect that this is the case the remedy is to try to key out the plant in manuals treating the plants of adjacent areas or send a specimen to some expert botanist for checking.

HINTS ON USING KEYS.

The way to attain proficiency in keying plants is to practice continuously. Even when the work of the day occupies your daylight hours there will usually be a few minutes in the evening when you can check over some of the plants picked up during the day. It is as easy to become "rusty" in identifying plants as it is in almost any kind of skill. An experienced botanist uses several "tricks" to help him get around certain difficulties in a key. Some of these are listed below.

1. Look the whole plant over in a general way before you start keying it. The alternative would be to deal with each character as it appears in the key.

2. Check yourself at every possible step with the descriptions. For example, when you arrive at a family in the key take time to read over the family description before proceeding. This may save you a lot of back tracking later on.

3. Run the plant both ways in doubtful cases. In the incorrect way the key usually begins to read all wrong. For example, you may meet a place where your only 2 choices are "Flowers red", as opposed to "Flowers yellow". If your plant has blue flowers you might conclude you have tried the wrong road. Or you may run the plant down to

a certain species and upon consulting the specific description find that it just will not fit. But on trying the correct path, the key begins to read right and the descriptions fit better.

In a long key several of these alternate "trials" can be made. Very often a positive identification can be secured with this method when for one reason or another it is impossible to make positive choices at several places in the key.

4. If your manual has pictures or drawings of the species, use them to check your identification. It is seldom possible to identify a plant by thumbing through these figures since the specific differences may be based on characters that cannot be shown in a drawing. Remember a drawing is a static thing but the individuals constituting a species are not. A good description is far superior to a drawing to illustrate this range of variability. For that reason most manuals do not try to illustrate each species. Pictures ought to illustrate the diagnostic visual characters. An excellent way to use them is to check the visual characters used in the key by referring to pictured examples under each category. Remember that your plant can actually look more like the figure of species number one when it may actually be species number two! The key and description should have the final word on the subject.

5. Learn to weigh and evaluate the important characters in cases of doubt. Usually the floral structures have more importance than vegetative ones. For example, if your plant has the correct flower length for one species but fits better under another for height of plant you would do much better in giving the greater weight to the floral character.

6. Use your knowledge of the group to help. This comes only with experience. An experienced worker is constantly reasoning something like this, "My plant cannot be this species because I am familiar with it and it is much different, therefore I must take the other road in the key."

7. Check your final determination by reference to the recorded habitat. The habitat is the local condition under which a plant grows. If a description ends by saying "plants of wet soil, borders of ponds and marshes", and your plant came from a dry hilltop, you are justified in suspecting your identification. This must be done with caution as your manual may give incomplete or even faulty information on the matter.

8. Check your identification by reference to the recorded locality. If your manual excludes your state for the species, perhaps even by the interval of several states, you have a right to suspect your identification. Again this must be done with caution especially with weedy plants. Even with native plants new information is constantly accumulating concerning this distribution.

Chapter XIII

COLLECTING AND PRESSING PLANTS

VALUES OF COLLECTING AND PRESSING PLANTS.

1. One of the very best ways to learn plants is to
    collect and press them. Otherwise when many
    plants are identified the later ones tend to
    crowd out the earlier ones in your mind. But if
    you save a specimen you can refer to it constant-
    ly. Each time you change blotters as explained
    below, write out a label or fix the plant to the
    sheet, you get a chance to see the specimen.

    The plant looks different in the field as it
    grows but consulting your specimen is an excel-
    lent way to recall to memory its appearance. If
    you have pressed the plant yourself you know
    what happens in the process. Many botanists can
    look at their specimens and recall to mind the
    exact appearance of almost every one as it looked
    when collected. One such botanist who had col-
    lected thousands of specimens over a period of 50
    years claimed that by looking at the pressed
    plants he was able to remember the exact details
    of every collection.

2. Collecting and pressing allows for securing large
    numbers of plants when the opportunity occurs,
    and identifying them later when more time is
    available. Many botanists spend all summer col-
    lecting specimens during daylight hours, putting
    them in presses during the evenings, then iden-
    tifying and mounting them during the winter.
    With such a procedure it is surprising how many
    plants can be dealt with in a season.

3. By collecting the plant you have an opportunity
    of checking up on your identification by sub-
    mitting the specimen to an authority. If pos-
    sible collect duplicate material and keep one
    specimen for yourself. Almost any expert is
    willing to check material for you if your plants
    are well collected, well pressed and have com-
    plete and dependable data attached. His payment

is a good specimen of the plant for his collection.

4. A set of named specimens will often prove useful
to aid in checking the identity of later col-
lections by comparison. It is seldom possible
to actually identify a plant from the beginning
by leafing over a collection since so many
species are involved. But it does allow for
checking your determination or helping decide between possibilities. Be certain your pressed
plant is correctly named and remember that two
individuals of a species may not look exactly
alike. The comparison should be made on the
basis of the important diagnostic characters
used in the group concerned. It is possible
that the individual plant you are checking may
actually resemble more closely in general appearance a specimen of the wrong species than it
does of the correct one!

5. A collection of plant specimens provides an au-
thentic record of the species of an area.
Every printed list of plants ought to be backed
up in this concrete fashion. If anyone doubts
your identification of a particular plant you
can always refer him to your specimen.

GENERAL DIRECTIONS FOR COLLECTING PLANTS.

1. Select an average plant or collect several specimens showing the range of variation. Remember
that your specimen is to be representative of
the species in that area. There is a temptation
to collect "freaks" or "off color" plants as
oddities but if you do so, be sure to state the
situation clearly on the label.

2. Collect the plant in flower if possible. In
special groups where rather mature fruit is
necessary, like the Cruciferae (mustard family)
or Umbelliferae (carrot family) look around and
try to find a plant with both flowers and fruit
present. Sometimes you may find one plant in
flower and another in fruit and the two can be
mounted together.

3. Collect all the plant when possible, including the underground parts, especially if these are unusual in some way (such as bulbs, corms, rhizomes, etc.). In any case collect enough to give a clue as to the annual or perennial habit of a herbaceous plant. The roots of woody plants are seldom collected, however.

A large plant can be bent or folded to fit your equipment. With a very large plant certain representative portions can be selected; these parts will usually be the flowers and leaves. Avoid selecting very small plants; they may fit your mounting sheet but may not be representative of the species.

4. Place the plant at once in the press, vasculum or collecting can. This is particularly important in arid regions. A really good specimen is impossible to make from a wilted plant.

5. Keep accurate information about each plant; better use a field notebook rather than to depend on memory alone. All or most of this data will appear on the label so it must be accurate. An inaccurate or misplaced label can cause trouble and confusion for years and even centuries. The information you may need for your label is listed below.

(1.) Absolutely necessary information.

    A. The habitat or local conditions under which a plant grows. In mountainous areas the altitude where the collection was made is important.

    B. The locality, preferably by reference to a town, county and state. Such information should allow someone else to find the approximate area if they wish. Very local names like "Happy Hollow" or "Smith's Ranch", should not be used, at least alone. By referring to a county and town anyone consulting your specimen can figure out the exact locality from a map. Even when the town has ceased to exist, it will still be recorded on older maps.

C. The day, month and year of collection.

D. The name of the collector.

(2.) <u>Very desirable information.</u>

    A. Color of the flowers. This may be partly or completely obscured in the pressing.

    B. Height of the plant if only a portion is collected. This is particularly important in dealing with woody plants such as shrubs and trees. The type of branching may be worth recording especially if it is unusual. For example, you may not be able to tell from a pressed specimen whether the stem was decumbent or ascending.

    C. Technical information you need to identify plants in that group but which does not show up well on pressed material. For example, in the genus <u>Castilleja</u> (paint brushes) one may need to know if the calyx is cut deeper above or below in order to key out the species. By recording this information you later save yourself and others the bother of detaching and soaking up a flower.

(3.) <u>Special information you may need yourself.</u>

    This may be almost anything but may include some of the following.

    A. Ecological information such as plant formation, soil type, etc.

    B. Economic importance such as grazing value, importance as a weed, use in medicine, etc.

    C. Relative abundance in the locality.

    D. Field variations observed.

    E. Insect visitors to the plant.

    F. A photograph of the plant to be pasted on the mounting sheet along with the label.

EQUIPMENT FOR COLLECTING PLANTS.

These vary with the individual. Every experienced collector has certain pet tools and gad-
gets suited to his particular needs or tempera-
ment. The following list is almost essential.

1. Digging tool. This may be variable but should
be painted some bright color to aid in locating
it if it is forgotten. In the photograph A.
is a hand pick, B. is a small trowel-like digger
while C. is a strong hunting knife. If possible
try them all before selecting one. Better yet
construct for yourself the ideal one! Fig. 211.

Fig. 211.

2. Sharp knife. This is to cut off parts such as
twigs of woody plants. A pocket knife does very
well.

3. Container. This is for storing the plants until
    they can be put away in the presses. The object
    is to prevent undue wilting. On cold days
    plants may be kept all day in excellent condition
    in a vasculum. A. is a hand press, B. is a vas-
    culum, C. is a lard can and D. is an ordinary
    plant press. Fig. 212.

Fig. 212.

    The vasculum can be carried around, the
lard can may be used as a central storehouse.
Many botanists do not use any collecting can at
all but place the plant at once in a temporary
press called a hand press (Fig. 212A.). This usually consists of many single sheets of paper
within a stiff cover like wallboard, the whole
supported by straps attached to a handle for convenience in carrying.

4. Conveyance. Automobile, train, horse, bicycle,
    boat or walking. The wide use of the automobile
    has resulted in a great deal of roadside collect-
    ing. The most interesting areas for finding un-
    usual plants often lie away from the highways.

SOURCES FOR COLLECTING EQUIPMENT.

Many of the implements mentioned above can be found at your local stores. A vasculum can be constructed by your local tinsmith. A few supply houses are given below in case you wish to purchase these items.

1. General Biological Supply House, 8200 South Hoyne Avenue, Chicago, Illinois.

2. Wards Natural Science Establishment Inc., 3000 Ridge Road East, Rochester 9, New York.

DIRECTIONS FOR PRESSING PLANTS.

1. Give each plant a number, these numbers running in consecutive order through the lifetime of the collector. This number corresponds to that used in the Field Notebook.

2. Place the plant in a once-folded paper cover approximately $16\frac{1}{2}$ x $11\frac{1}{2}$ inches in size. An ordinary newspaper sheet will make this folder, in addition it may provide someone with interesting reading 40 or 50 years later! The number of the plant is placed on the paper folder and this stays with the specimen throughout the process.

3. Arrange the plant so that the floral parts are well displayed. It may be necessary to bend the stem once or more times and remove some leaves.

4. Place this folder with its specimen between thick blotters of about the same size (18 x 12 inches works very well). If blotters are not available you can use all or part of a folded newspaper which acts as a blotter. A board is placed on the pile and a weight is placed on top. A flat stone does very well if it weighs about 20 or 30 lbs. A conventional plant press is made up of 2 boards, often latticed, with straps or ropes around them, and this can be readily transported (Fig. 212 D.).

5. Replace these blotters with dry ones as needed. The wet ones can be dried out and used again later. Plants with watery thick parts may dry slowly. A good rule is to change blotters every 24 hours for two or three times, then every 48

hours until the plant has been pressed flat and is perfectly dry. You soon learn by experience how long this period will be. If you are in a hurry or the air is humid and moist, it is necessary to use artificial heat. Corrugated cardboards (or aluminum corrugates sold by supply houses) are inserted among the plant sheets and the press is suspended over a heat source. Of course the heat must not be too intense. Botanists often have a special box constructed that contains a heating unit and a fan at the base.

6. Secure thin cardboard sheets $11\frac{1}{2}$ x $16\frac{1}{2}$ inches in size. Ordinary thin paper does not hold its shape very well but very thick cardboard takes up too much space. These sheets can be secured from a paper supply company or can be ordered from a biological supply house (see list in this chapter).

7. Glue the specimens to this sheet or fasten them with strips of gummed cloth. Many botanists use a tin paste for this purpose but ordinary glue does very well. Recently strips of liquid plastic have been used to hold down the specimen. Gummed paper may become brittle in time as is the case with scotch tape. Often both gluing and stripping are used. The strips are placed in a fashion to prevent the plant from slipping lengthwise out of the fasteners. Leave space at the lower righthand corner for the label.

8. The labels should be about 3 x $4\frac{1}{2}$ inches in size or somewhat smaller. You can have them printed with your name if you wish. Space should be available for the necessary information and anything else of a special nature. These labels are for sale at the biological supply houses.

9. Store the plants so that they are accessible. The usual way is to place the species of a genus in a folded cardboard cover, these genera are arranged by families. Such folders can be stored in cabinets or cases. A constant watch should be kept to prevent damage from insects. These pests may actually breed in the cases and the larvae can soon ruin a collection. Some

botanists fumigate the material periodically with Hydrocyanic Acid fumes or other insecticides of similar nature. Paradichlorobenzine flakes may act as a repellent or spraying at intervals with a DDT solution may protect the plants. An insect tight case is of course desirable to keep out these pests.

Chapter XIV

MANUALS AND FLORAS

Wherever you may go in the United States you will
find that a manual or flora has been written for i-
dentifying the plants of that area. Some of these
books are rather old, others are new and up-to-date
in nomenclature and treatment. Unfortunately many
are now out of print and must be obtained by borrow-
ing from libraries or by purchasing from dealers in
secondhand books.

Only the more important manuals and floras are
listed in this chapter, and the list is limited to
those treating the plants of Alaska, Canada and the
United States. If you wish to identify plants from
other countries of the world or wish a more complete
list of manuals or floras consult the following
sources.

1. Blake, S. F. and Atwood, A. C. Geographical
    Guide to Floras of the World. Part I.
    U. S. D. A. Misc. Pub. 401. 1942.

        This first part deals with Africa,
    Australasia, Insular Floras, North America and
    South America. The second part of this useful
    work will cover Asia and Europe.

2. Lawrence, G. H. M. Taxonomy of the Vascular
    Plants. The MacMillan Company, New York, N. Y.
    1951.

        Chapter XIV deals with the Literature of
    Systematic Botany and gives the more important
    manuals and floras of the various continents
    and islands of the world.

3. Blake, S. F. Guide to Popular Floras of the
    United States and Alaska. U. S. D. A. Biblio-
    graphical Bulletin No. 23. June, 1954.

        Many of the "popular" floras listed are
    based on careful and continuous study of the
    plants of the area covered. They may contain

diagnostic keys very useful in identifying the plants. Often they treat special groups, such as the woody plants of the area, using characters of twig and leaf which allows for the identification of these plants before or after the flowering period.

4. Core, E. L. Plant Taxonomy. Prentice Hall, Inc. 1955.

    Chapter XI deals with the literature of Systematic Botany.

WORLD.

1. Bentham, G. and Hooker, J. D. Genera Plantarum. 3 volumes. London. 1862-1883.

    In Latin. Devoted to the genera of seed plants, grouped under families. No formal keys are given but the major groupings are separated by synoptical devices. No attempt is made of course to provide means for identifying the species.

2. Engler, A. and Prantl, K. Die naturlichen Pflanzenfamilien. 23 volumes. Leipzig. 1887-1915; edition 2, 1924 - Incomplete (1957).

    In German. This treats the families and genera of the world (except the Bacteria). It is well illustrated and carries the classification down to the genera with keys to the major groupings. The second edition promises to be of special value to students of the world flora.

UNITED STATES - SPECIAL GROUPS.

    These books treat a particular group of plants over a wide area. In addition monographs and revisions of certain taxonomic groups may be available. These usually treat a particular genus as represented in a certain geographical area. Often this area may be the United States or North America. If you know the genus then these monographs can be used to determine the species. Unfortunately most such treatments are unavailable to the average student, scattered as they are through various periodicals.

No attempt is made to list these numerous works here.
The pertinent information from these monographs
eventually becomes incorporated in the manuals and
floras listed later on in this chapter.

1. Grasses

    1. Hitchcock, A. S. Manual of the Grasses of
       the United States. Second edition revised
       by Agnes Chase, U. S. D. A. Misc. Pub. 200.
       Washington, D. C. 1951.

           An illustrated treatment of the family
       Gramineae (Poaceae) as represented in the
       United States. It is based on the huge
       grass collection assembled at the U. S.
       National Herbarium. The species are illus-
       trated and described.

2. Cultivated plants

    1. Bailey, L. H. Manual of Cultivated Plants.
       Edition 2. 1116 pages. The MacMillan Co.,
       New York. 1949.

           The plants commonly grown in the United
       States and Canada are keyed out and describ-
       ed. The general arrangement is similar to
       the manuals with which the student is famil-
       iar. Single citations only are given for
       the scientific names.

    2. Bailey, L. H. The Standard Cyclopedia of
       Horticulture. 6 vols. 1914-1917. (The
       second edition of 1922 was re-issued in 1935
       in 3 volumes.)

           Provides keys to and descriptions of
       the plants commonly cultivated in the United
       States and Canada with information as to
       their culture and use. The first volume con-
       tains a synopsis of the plant kingdom with a
       key to the families and genera. The genera
       are arranged alphabetically throughout the
       rest of the work. The family key is diffi-
       cult for students and the work as a whole is
       bulky and hard to transport. For that reason
       the smaller Bailey's Manual is recommended
       for ordinary use in identifying cultivated
       plants.

3.   Rehder, Alfred. Manual of Cultivated Trees
     and Shrubs. 825 pages. Second edition
     1940. MacMillan Co.

          This book is on the order of a regular
     manual with keys and descriptions to the
     woody plants grown in North America. The
     keys are based on floral characters. Since
     most of the common native woody plants have
     been in cultivation at one time or another,
     the publication is very useful for identify-
     ing the general flora.

3. **Trees**

   1.   Sargent, C. S. Manual of the Trees of North
        America Exclusive of Mexico. Illustrated.
        Second Edition. Houghton-Mifflin Co., 1922.

             Provides keys to families, genera and
        species. In addition the species are des-
        cribed and illustrated. Really an abridg-
        ment of the author's 14 volume set called
        "The Silva of North Ameria" which is usually
        unavailable to the average student.

UNITED STATES - GENERAL FLORA.

1. Britton, N. L., et al. North American Flora.
    Published by the New York Botanical Garden.
    1905 - not completed (1957).

         Planned in 34 volumes and will include all
    the native plants of North American from bacteria
    and algae through the seed plants. The work to
    date has been done by various specialists of the
    groups concerned but under a uniform editorial
    policy. Prior to 1935 the American Code of
    Nomenclature was followed, since that time the
    International Rules have been used. If the par-
    ticular family or genus is recognized by the
    student and has been treated in this publication
    to date then the work would be a valuable aid to
    the student in identification of plants. Usually
    the complete manuals and floras covering a more
    limited area will be more useful.

UNITED STATES - MANUALS AND FLORAS.

These publications are designed to allow you to identify the native plants of a certain designated area. They may include keys only but most of them have family, generic and specific descriptions of varying completeness. When descriptions are given the book is likely to be called a "manual", when they are lacking it may be designated a "flora" but this practice is not uniform. Unfortunately many of these manuals and floras are out of print and a few are as yet incomplete. When an area is very inadequately covered by a regional manual then more local floras may be listed here.

A.   Northeastern United States

   1.   Fernald, M. L.   Gray's Manual of Botany. Eighth Edition, 1632 pages.   American Book Co.   1950.   Map I. 6 and IV. 3.

        Although designated as a revision this edition is essentially a new work.   It is one volume and although rather bulky can still be easily carried around.   For this and other reasons "Gray's Manual" has been the favorite text for classes in its area for many years.   Some of the species are accompanied by small drawings, these usually of some diagnostic portion.   Accepted varieties are listed and often a key is presented to them.   This increases the size of the publication and may not be of a special value to the beginning student.   However, they add to the authoritativeness and completeness and can be ignored if desired. The flora of adjacent Canada is included (See Canadian Floras).

   2.   Gleason, H.   The New Britton and Brown Illustrated Flora of the Northeastern United States and Adjacent Canada.   New York Botanical Garden.   1952.   3 volumes.   Map I. 6 and III. 3.

        The 3 volumes are rather bulky to carry in the field, and this fact combined with the necessary higher cost has resulted in the work being used more largely as a

reference than as a text. The keys and
descriptions are reasonably complete. Each
species is illustrated and the diagnostic
structure is usually indicated, often by enlarging a portion of the plant. Although it
is stated in the preface that the work "has
been prepared primarily for the interested
laity rather than the professional botanist",
the publication remains a technical manual.

The new edition is a revision of the
Britton and Brown Illustrated Flora, Second
Edition, 1913. The older edition differed
from the new by including citations to orig-
inal sources and by including the states of
Kansas, Nebraska, South Dakota and North
Dakota to the west. The older work also ex-
tended much farther north into Canada (See
Canadian Floras).

B. Southeastern and Southcentral United States

1. Small, J. K. Manual of the Southeastern
Flora. 1933. Published by the Author.
New York. 1370 pages. Map I. 7.

A conventional manual with keys and
descriptions of seed plants (the ferns not
included). The floral characters of each
genus are illustrated. Although published
after 1930 when the followers of the 2 codes
finally reconciled their differences, unfortunately the nomenclature still follows
closest to the American Code Rules instead of
the now generally used International Rules.

2. Small, J. K. Flora of the Southeastern
United States. Second Edition 1913. Published by the Author. New York. 1,394
pages. Map II. 4.

This is the work on which the preceding
revision was based. It is important still
because it differs from the newer version as
follows. (a) It includes the Pteriodophyta.
(b) It extends west to the 100th meridian
and accordingly includes Arkansas, Louisiana,
most of Oklahoma and over one-half of Texas

(west of the eastern border of the Texas Panhandle). The American Code of Nomenclature is followed.

3. Stemen, T. R. and Myers, W. S. Oklahoma Flora. Harlow Publishing Co. 1937. 706 pages.

   Manual-like is the pattern with some of the species illustrated. The descriptions are short and the families Cyperaceae and Gramineae are omitted. The American Code of Nomenclature is followed.

4. Reeves, R. G. and Bain, D. C. Flora of Southcentral Texas. W. M. Wetch Manufacturing Company, Chicago, Ill. 1947. 298 pages.

   A rather abbreviated manual covering an irregular area in the Costal Plains of Texas from Madison County extending southwest to Bee and Guadaloupe Counties. The treatment of the grasses is admittedly incomplete and the Pteridophytes are omitted altogether.

   At this writing the flora of Texas is very inadequately treated in any form. A Flora of Texas is in preparation and several parts have been issued to date. It is published by the Southern Methodist University, University Press, Dallas, Texas.

C. Midwestern United States

1. Rydberg, P. A. Flora of the Prairies and Plains of Central North America. New York Bot. Garden. New York. 1932. 969 pages. Map II. 3.

   A conventional manual with keys and descriptions. Many of the genera have one species illustrated. The nomenclature follows the International Rules. A small portion of southcentral Canada is included. (See Canadian Floras.)

105

2. Stevens, O. A. Handbook of North Dakota Plants. Fargo, North Dakota. 1950. 324 pages.

Contains keys to families, genera and species with rather brief descriptions of each, except in genera with very few species. Many plants are illustrated and some of the characters used in the main family key are accompanied by marginal drawings.

D. Western United States

1. Coulter, J. and Nelson, A. New Manual of Botany of the Central Rocky Mountains (vascular plants). American Book Co. 1909. 646 pages. Map I. 4.

The keys and descriptions were kept rather short which allowed this book to be a size convenient for carrying around. The nomenclature follows the International Rules. A so-called conservative attitude is adopted in the treatment of specific units.

2. Rydberg, P. A. Flora of the Rocky Mountains and Adjacent Plains, Colorado, Utah, Wyoming, Idaho, Montana, Saskatchewan, Alberta and neighboring Parts of Nebraska, South Dakota, North Dakota and British Columbia. Published by the Author. New York. Second Edition 1922. 1143 pages. Map II. 2 and III. 2.

This second edition contains 33 pages of additions and corrections but is otherwise like the first. The American Code of Nomenclature is followed and the Author was what some people call a "splitter", often dividing the older "species" into several to many. For that reason students may find this manual difficult to use.

3. Tidestrom, I. and Kittell, Sister, T. A Flora of Arizona and New Mexico. Catholic University of America Press. Washington, D. C. 1941. 897 pages.

This publication presents keys to the families, genera and species. In addition very abbreviated specific descriptions are often given. The arrangement of the families is unconventional with the Gymnosperms, Dicotyledons and Monocotyledons presented in that order, ending with the Pteridophytes.

4. Kearney, T. H. and Peebles, R. H. Arizona Flora. University of California Press. 1951. 1032 pages.

    Contains keys to the families, genera and species of Arizona plants with descriptions to the families and genera only. The keys are exceptionally complete and accurate but are of the bracket instead of the indented type, and therefore harder for most botanists to use. The publication supercedes the Author's "Flowering Plants and Ferns of Arizona" 1942.

5. Harrington, H. D. Manual of the Plants of Colorado. Sage Books, Denver, Colorado 1954. 666 pages.

    Gives keys to families, genera and species. Each species is accompanied by a complete specific description as well as the geographical and altitudinal range within the State.

6. Tidestrom, I. Flora of Utah and Nevada. Contr. U. S. Herb. Vol. 25. 665 pages. 1925.

    Provides the usual keys to families, genera and species but descriptions to the families only. The nomenclature follows the American Code.

7. Porter, C. L. Contributions Toward a Flora of Wyoming. Issued in numbered leaflets. University of Wyoming.

    These are mostly mimeographed (or with some similar process) each treating one family. The family description is usually accompanied by one or more diagrams or

107

drawings illustrating the floral type. The genera are described but not the species. The work is incomplete to date (1957).

8. Piper, Chas. V. Flora of the State of Washington. Contr. U. S. Nat. Herb. Vol. 11. 1906. 637 pages.

   Keys to families, genera and species are presented but no descriptions are given except to the newly described species. A list of "specimens examined" is given for each species. The nomenclature used is closest to the rules adopted by the followers of the American Code.

9. St. John, Harold. Flora of Southeastern Washington and Adjacent Idaho. Student's Book Corporation. Pullman, Washington 1937. 476 pages. Map I. 3.

   Besides the usual keys this book has descriptions to the families, genera and species. The nomenclature follows the International Rules. An interesting feature is the alphabetical arrangement of the genera under the families, and the species under the genera. This is designed to make each taxon easier to locate.

10. Holmgren, A. H. Handbook of the Vascular Plants of Northeastern Nevada. Utah State Agri. College and U. S. Grazing Service. 1942. 214 pages. Mimeographed. Map I. 2.

    Contains keys to the families, genera and species with short descriptions to the genera only. The nomenclature follows the International Rules. The study includes all of Elko County and the northern parts of Eureka and Lander Counties.

11. Davis, Ray. Flora of Idaho. Wm. D. Brown Company, Dubuque, Iowa. 1952. 828 pages.

    This is manual-like with keys and descriptions to all the taxa. The specific descriptions are reasonably complete. An

unusual feature of this work is that the
genera in each family and the species under
the genera are alphabetically arranged.

12. Peck, M. E. A Manual of the Higher Plants
     of Oregon. Benfords and Mort. Portland,
     Oregon. 1941. 866 pages.

          This book gives keys to and descrip-
     tions of the families, genera and species
     of the state. The descriptions are reason-
     ably complete and local description within
     the state is given.

13. Abrams, L. An Illustrated Flora of the
     Pacific States, Washington, Oregon and
     California. Stanford Univ. Press. 3 Vols.
     1940-1951. (4th Volume to be issued.)
     Map II. 2.

          The first volume was originally issued
     in 1923 but in 1940 was revised to conform
     with the International Rules of Nomencla-
     ture. The 4th volume will contain the fam-
     ily keys. The generic and specific keys,
     as well as the family, generic and specific
     descriptions are very complete. Each
     species is accompanied by an illustration,
     many original but often borrowed from the
     Britton and Brown's Illustrated Flora. The
     4 volumes (when the last is completed) will
     be rather bulky to carry in the field but
     will be invaluable as a source of reference.

14. Jepson, W. L. A Manual of the Flowering
     Plants of California. Univ. of California,
     Berkeley, Calif. 1923-1925. 1238 pages.

          A conventional manual with keys and
     descriptions. Certain species are accompan-
     ied by illustrations, these well done. The
     Pteridophytes are included in the work.

          A later book by the same author is the
     "Flora of California" projected in 3 vol-
     umes. This is a more authoritative work
     with bibliographic references but is not as
     yet completed.

15. Munz, P. A. A Manual of Southern California Botany. J. W. Stacey, Inc. San Fran-
cisco. 1935. 642 pages. Map I. 1.

This is a regular manual with keys and
descriptions of the families, genera and
species of California south of a line from
Point Conception in Santa Barbara to north
of Death Valley on the east. Many of the
species are illustrated.

ALASKA AND CANADA - MANUALS AND FLORAS

1. Hulten, E. The Flora of the Aleutian Is-
lands and Westernmost Alaska Peninsula, with
Notes on the Flora of Commander Islands.
Stockholm. 1937. 397 pages.

A well annotated list of the species
included with detailed distributional in-
information. No keys or descriptions of the
477 species are provided.

2. Hulten, E. Flora of Alaska and Yukon.
Lunds univ. arssk. N. F. Avd. Lund. 1941-
1950. Parts I.-X. Map III. 1.

This is an annotated flora with keys
to species but with no keys to the larger
groups. No descriptions are included but
full synonomy and local distributional data
are presented including distributional maps
for each species. Notes concerning variations, differences from related species etc.
accompany many of the species.

3. Anderson, J. P. Flora of Alaska and Adjacent Parts of Canada. An illustrated
descriptive text of all vascular plants
known to occur within the region covered.
Iowa State College Journal of Science
Volume 18, 19, 20, 21, 23, 24, 26. 1943-
1952. Map IV. 1.

Presents keys to and descriptions of
the families, genera and species. Most
species are illustrated by original drawings. The parts of Canada covered are the
Yukon Territory and the extreme northwestern

110

part of British Columbia. This work was issued in parts but may be gathered together
in book form in the future.

4. Taylor, R. F. and E. L. Little, Jr. Pocket
Guide to Alaska Trees. U. S. D. A. Forest
Service, Agri. Handbook No. 55. June, 1950.
63 pages.

Semi-popular in nature but very useful.
Contains descriptions and illustrations of
30 species of trees with the distribution of
each given. The key to the species is based
mainly on vegetative characters. A winter
key to the deciduous trees is presented and
some selected references are listed at the
end of the booklet. It is of pocket size
and should be very useful to the student of
Alaskan trees.

5. Macoun, J. Catalogue of Canadian Plants.
Geol. and Nat. Hist. Survey of Canada. 3
Volumes, 7 parts. Montreal, Canada. 1883-
1902.

An annotated list of the phanerogams
and cryptogams of Canada including Alaska
and Newfoundland. Parts I-V (Volumes 1-2),
deals with 3209 species of vascular plants.
No keys are included and descriptions are
given to only a relatively few species but
the information on local and general distribution is fairly complete. The work would
hardly allow for student identification but
would be of value as a check list of possibilities.

6. Forestry Branch. Native Trees of Canada.
Bulletin 61. 4th Edition 1950. Dept. of
Resources and Development, Canada.

Gives descriptions to native species
with photographs of habit, leaves, fruits
etc. The local distribution is given on a
map for each species. No keys are presented
and the book is semi-popular in nature.

111

7. Louis-Marie, Pere. Flore-manuel de la pro-
vince due quebec. 319 pages. Montreal,
Canada. 1931. (Contrib. No. 23. Institut
d'Oka).

  Elementary flora of the vascular plants
of Quebec, in the form of keys. Text in
French.

8. Marie-Victorin, Frere. Flore laurentienne.
917 pages. Montreal, Canada. 1935. Map
III. 4.

  An annotated, illustrated descriptive
flora of vascular plants, with keys. The
text is in French. The area covered is in
southern Quebec north to about Lake St.
John.

9. Fernald, M. L. Gray's Manual of Botany.
8th Edition. 1632 pages. American Book Co.,
1950. Map IV. 3.

  The 8th Edition includes southern Ontario and Quebec south of the 49th parallel
of latitude and all of New Brunswick, Nova
Scotia, Prince Edward Island and Newfoundland.

10. Gleason, H. The New Britton and Brown Il-
lustrated Flora of the Northeastern United
States and Adjacent Canada. New York
Botanical Garden. 1952. 3 volumes. Map
III. 3.

  This includes southern Ontario from a
point east of Lake Superior and east along
the 47th parallel latitude to the St.
Lawrence River and all the area south of that
river except Newfoundland.

11. Rydberg, P. A. Flora of the Prairies and
Plains of Central North America. New York
Botanical Garden. New York. 1932. 969
pages. Map IV. 2.

  This covers a small portion of southern
Manitoba and southeastern Saskatchewan.

12. Rydberg, P. A. Flora of the Rocky Moun-
    tains and Adjacent Plains, Colorado, Utah,
    Wyoming, Idaho, Montana, Saskatchewan,
    Alberta and Neighboring Parts of Nebraska,
    South Dakota, North Dakota and British
    Columbia. Published by the Author. New
    York. Second Edition 1922. 1143 pages.
    Map III. 2.

    This flora extends northward from the
    northwestern corner of Idaho to the 55th
    parallel latitude and then east to the
    eastern borders of Saskatchewan; then south
    to the United States. It includes the
    southern half of Saskatchewan and Alberta
    with a small strip of southeastern British
    Columbia.

13. Britton, N. L. and Brown, A. An Illustrated
    Flora of the Northern United States and
    Canada. Three Volumes. Chas. Scribner's
    Sons, New York. 1896. Second Edition 1913.
    Map V. 1.

    This covers eastern Canada from New-
    foundland and Labrador west to the eastern
    border of Saskatchewan. The revised edition
    of this work covers a more limited area in
    both Canada and the United States (See
    number 10).

Note: In the descriptive material opposite the 5
      maps the letter and number in parenthesis
      (example - D-15) refers to the place in this
      chapter where a discussion of the particular
      manual or flora can be found.

Map I.

1. Munz, P. A. A Manual of Southern California
    Botany. (D-15)

2. Holmgren, A. H. Handbook of the Vascular Plants
    of Northeastern Nevada. (D-10)

3. St. John, H. Flora of Southeastern Washington
    and Adjacent Idaho. (D-9)

4. Coulter, J. and Nelson, A. New Manual of Botany
    of the Central Rocky Mountains. (D-1)

5. Coulter, J. Botany of Western Texas. (Contrib.
    U. S. Natl. Herb. vol. 2. 1891-1894).

6. A. Fernald, M. L. Gray's Manual of Botany.
        (A-1)

    B. Gleason, H. The New Britton and Brown Il-
        lustrated Flora of the Northeastern United
        States and Adjacent Canada. (A-2)

7. Small, J. K. Manual of the Southeastern Flora.
    (B-1)

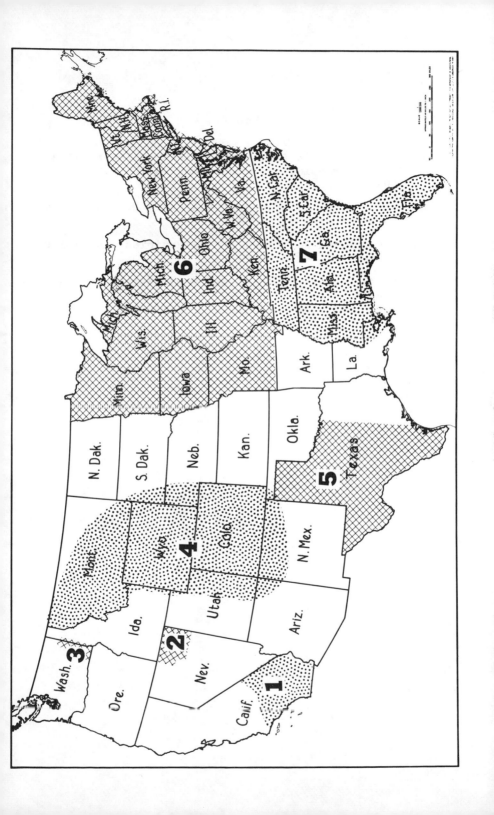

Map II.

1. Abrams, L. An Illustrated Flora of the Pacific States, Washington, Oregon and California. (D-13)

2. Rydberg, P. A. Flora of the Rocky Mountains and Adjacent Plains. (D-2)

3. Rydberg, P. A. Flora of the Prairies and Plains of Central North America. (C-1)

4. Small, J. K. Flora of the Southeastern United States. (B-2)

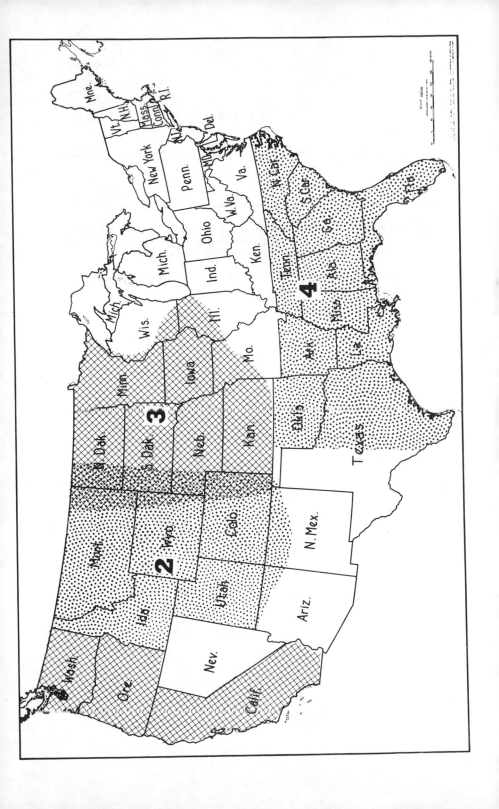

Map III.

1. Hulten, E. Flora of Alaska and Yukon. (Alaska and Canada - 2)

2. Rydberg, P. A. Flora of the Rocky Mountains and Adjacent Plains. (Alaska and Canada - 12; D-2)

3. Gleason, H. The New Britton and Brown Illustrated Flora of Northeastern United States and Canada. (Alaska and Canada - 10; A-2)

4. Marie-Victorin, Frere, Flore laurentienne. (Alaska and Canada - 8)

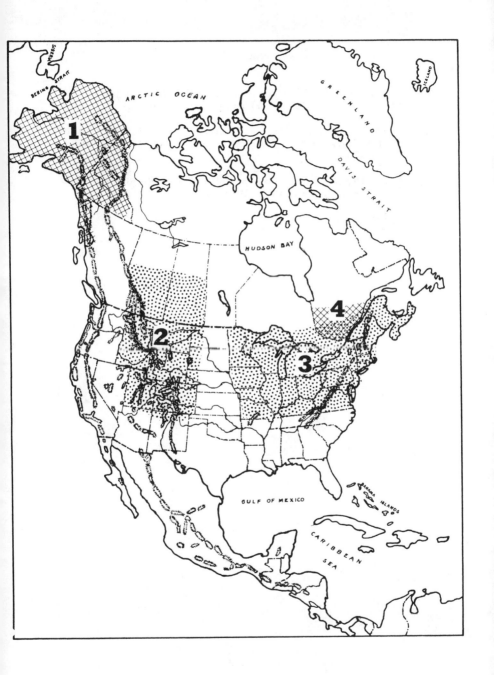

Map IV.

1. Anderson, J. P. Flora of Alaska and Adjacent
    Parts of Canada. (Alaska and Canada - 3)

2. Rydberg, P. A. Flora of the Prairies and Plains
    of Central North America. (Alaska and Canada -
    11; C-1)

3. Fernald, M. L. Gray's Manual of Botany.
    (Alaska and Canada - 9; A-1)

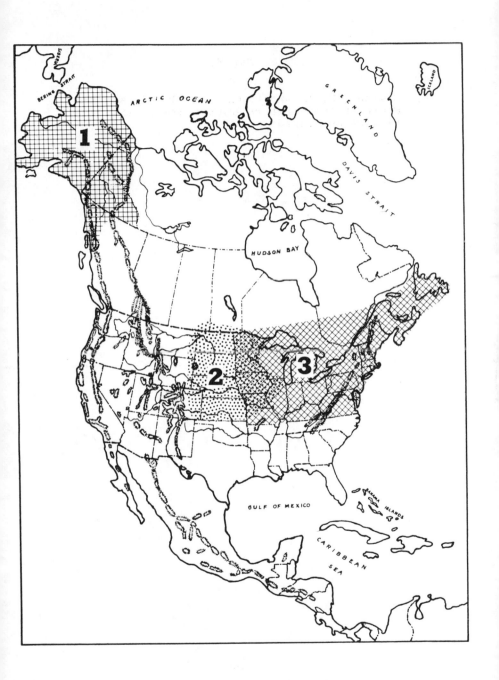

Map V.

1. Britton, N. L. and Brown, A. An Illustrated
    Flora of the Northern United States and Canada.
    (Alaska and Canada - 13)

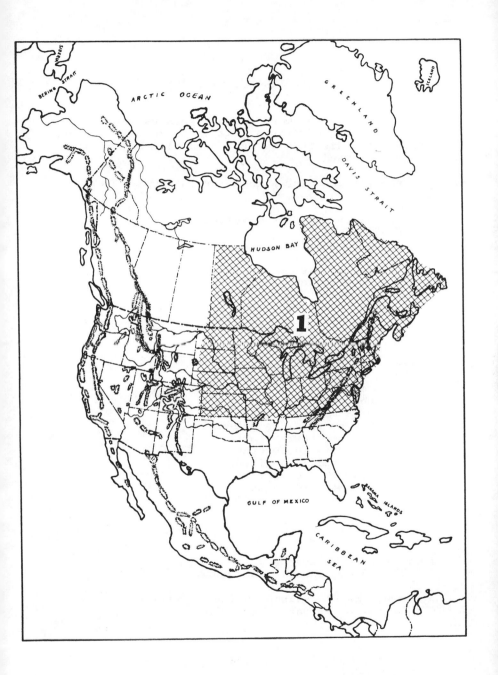

Chapter XV

ILLUSTRATED GLOSSARY

These are the more common terms used in the identification of plants. It is suggested that the preface to this book be read carefully before this chapter is used.

<u>A</u>. A prefix meaning without as in "apetalous".

Abortive. Imperfectly developed; rudimentary.

Acaulescent. Stemless or apparently so, or the stem subterranean; leaves basal or radical. Fig. 213.

ACAULESCENT
Fig. 213.

Accessory Fruit. A fleshy fruit with the fleshy part not a part of the pistil, like a strawberry where the receptacle is succulent and the ripened ovaries are achene-like. The drawings show such a fruit in surface view and split longitudinally with the achenes partly embedded in the fleshy receptacle, Fig. 214.

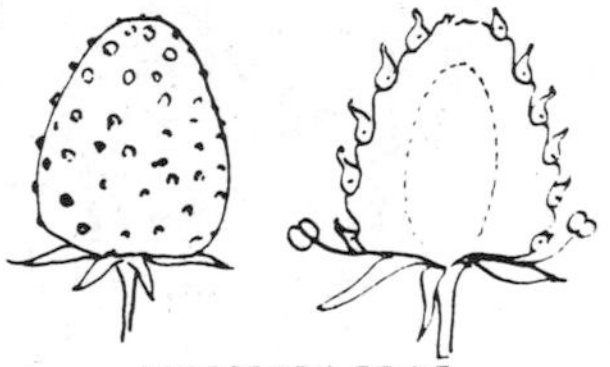

ACCESSORY FRUIT
Fig. 214.

Accrescent. Enlarging after flowering, usually the sepals.

Acerose. Needle-shaped as the leaves of spruce. Fig. 215.

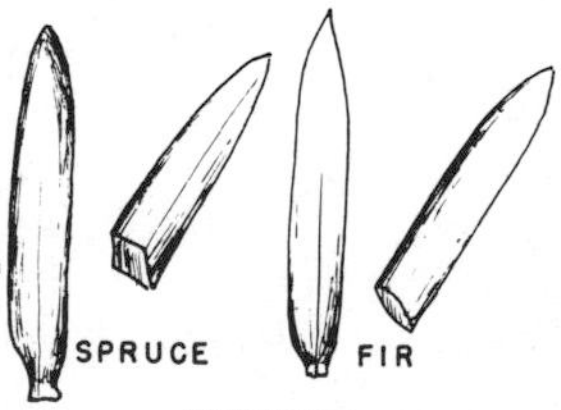

SPRUCE   FIR

ACEROSE
Fig. 215.

Achene. A small, dry, 1-celled, 1-
    seeded indehiscent fruit, the
    seed attached to the pericarp at
    1 place. Fig. 216.

ACHENE
Fig. 216.

Acicular. Shaped like a needle, as the
    "needle" of a pine tree. About the
    same as acerose.

Acorn. The 1-celled, 1-seeded fruit of
    oaks; consists of a cup-like base and
    the nut. Fig. 217.

ACORN OF OAK
Fig. 217.

Acrid. Sharp, irritating or biting to the taste.

Actinomorphic. Same as regular.

Acuminate. Tapering to the apex,
    the sides more or less pinch-
    ed in before reaching the
    tip. Compare acute.
    Fig. 218.

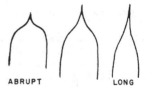

ACUMINATE
Fig. 218.

Acute. Tapering to the apex with the
    sides straight or nearly so; us-
    ually less tapering than acuminate.
    Fig. 219.

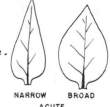

ACUTE
Fig. 219.

Adherent. Same as adnate.

Adnate. The union of unlike parts, as an inferior
    ovary to the calyx tube. Compare connate.

Adventitious. Developing in an unusual or irregular

125

position, usually used for roots.

Aerial. In the air, as roots borne above the ground
or water.

Aggregate. Crowded into a dense cluster but not
united.

Aggregate Fruit. A fleshy fruit
formed from several to many succulent pistils. The right-hand
figure shows such a fruit in
longitudinal section. Blackberry and raspberry are aggregate fruits. Fig. 220.

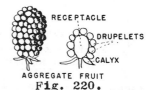

AGGREGATE FRUIT
Fig. 220.

Alpine. The area above timberline.

Alternate. Borne singly and not opposite - in leaves
one at a node. Fig. 221.

Alveolar. Honeycombed. See alveolate.

Alveolate. Honeycombed. Fig. 222.

Ament. A spike or spike-like, usually pendulous inflorescence of unisexual flowers. Same as
catkin. An ament would be either staminate or
pistillate. Fig. 223.

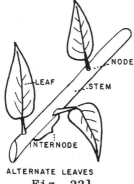

ALTERNATE LEAVES
Fig. 221.

ALVEOLATE
Fig. 222.

AMENT
Fig. 223.

Amphibious. Usually growing submerged but may sur-
vive for long periods outside of the water.

126

Ampliate. Enlarged.

Anatropous. Upturned or inverted, said of an ovule
 with its micropyle next to the funiculus.

Androecium. The collective name
 for the stamens.

Anemophilous. Having wind-borne
 pollen.

Annual. Completing the life
 cycle in one growing season.

Annular. In the form of a ring.
 Fig. 224.

ANNULAR EMBRYO
Fig. 224.

Annulate. In the form of a ring. See
 annular.

Anterior. On the front side away from the
 axis.

Anther. The pollen-bearing part of the
 stamen. Fig. 225.

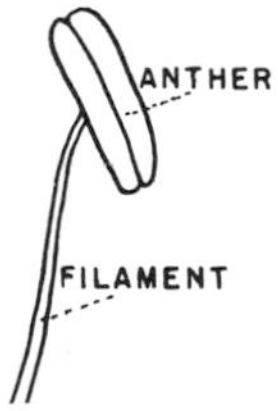

Fig. 225.

Anthesis. Period when the flower
 is open.

Antrorse. Directed forward or upward as of hairs. Fig. 226.

Apetalous. Lacking petals.

Apiculate. Ending in an abrupt
 slender tip which is not
 stiff. Fig. 227.

ANTRORSE HAIRS
Fig. 226.

Appendage. An attached secondary part to
 a main structure.

Appressed. Lying flat or close against
 something. Often used for hairs.

Approximate. Close together but not
 united.

APICULATE TIP
Fig. 227.

Aquatic. Living in water.

Arachnoid. Beset with cobwebby or en-
tangled hairs.

Arborescent. Approaching the size and
habit of a tree.

Arcuate. Arching or moderately curved
like a bow. Fig. 228.

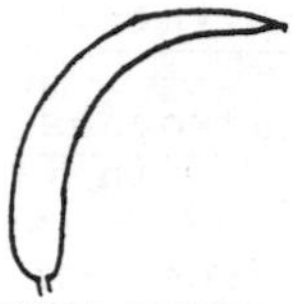

ARCUATE LEGUME
Fig. 228.

Areola (pl. areolae). A small
space marked out upon or beneath the surface; often used
in leaves for the area between small veins. Also
spelled areole. Fig. 229.

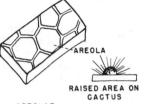

AREOLA

RAISED AREA ON
CACTUS

AREOLAE
Fig. 229.

Areole. See areola.

Aril. An appendage growing at or about the
hilum of a seed. Compare caruncle.

Aristate. With an awn or stiff bristle,
usually at the apex. Fig. 230.

ARISTATE TIP
Fig. 230.

Aristulate. Minutely aristate.

Armed. Provided with thorns, spines,
prickles or sharp hairs.

Articulating. With a joint or node
separating at maturity by a clean
cut scar.

Ascending. Growing obliquely upward,
often curving upward usually at
about 40° - 60°. Fig. 231.

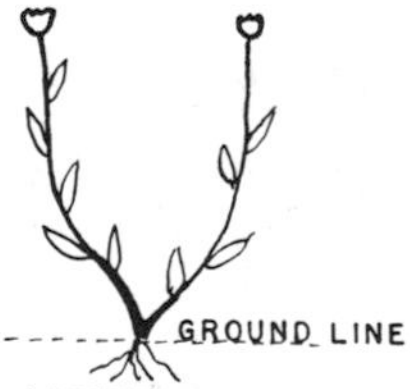

GROUND LINE

ASCENDING STEMS
Fig. 231.

Assurgent. Ascending.

Attenuate. Gradually narrowing to a tip
    or base, this usually narrow and
    slender. Fig. 232.

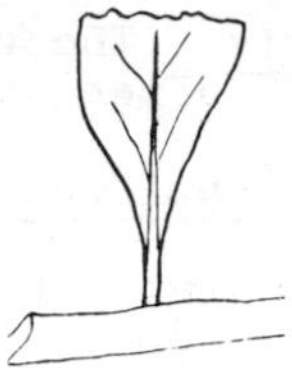

ATTENUATE
LEAF BASE
Fig. 232.

Auricle. An ear-shaped lobe or appendage. Fig. 233.

Auriculate. With auricles.

Awl-shaped. Tapering gradually upward from a broad-
    er base to a sharp point, narrowly triangular;
    usually used for small structures. Fig. 234.

Awn. A slender bristle-like organ usually at the
    apex of a structure. Fig. 235.

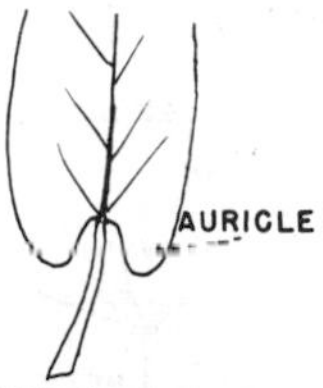

AURICLE

AURICLE AT BASE OF
LEAF BLADE
Fig. 233.

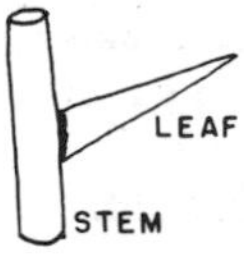

LEAF
STEM
AWL-SHAPED LEAF
Fig. 234.

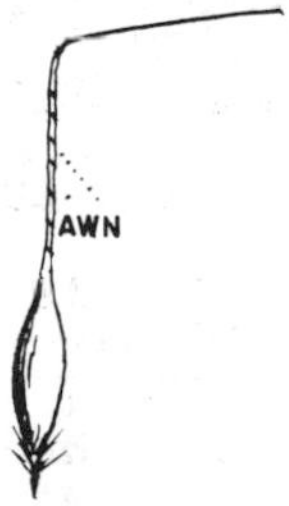

AWN
Fig. 235.

Axile. In the axil, the angle between an organ and
    its axis. See axillary.

Axile placentation. Ovules borne on the septum or
    septa of an ovary 2- or more- celled, usually
    near the center of the ovary. Fig. 236.

Axillary. In or related to the axis.
    Fig. 237.

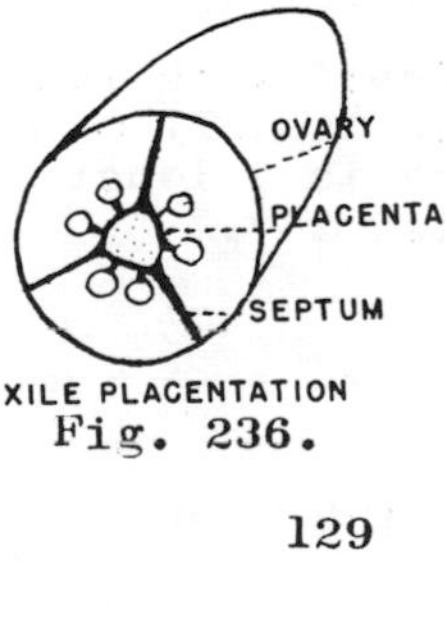

OVARY
PLACENTA
SEPTUM
AXILE PLACENTATION
Fig. 236.

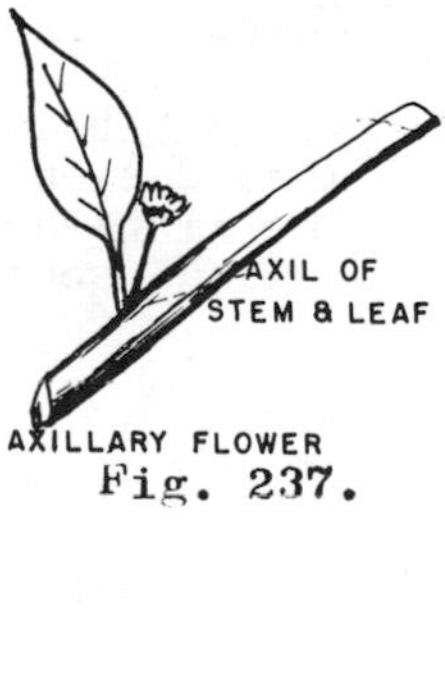

AXIL OF
STEM & LEAF
AXILLARY FLOWER
Fig. 237.

Axis. The elongated central supporting structure,
    often specifically called a rachis.

Balsamiferous. Sticky and odoriferous, like balsam.

Banner. The upper, usually larger petal in a papil-
    ionaceous or "sweetpea type" flower. Fig. 238.

Barbed. With rigid short reflexed processes, like
    the barb of a fishhook. The drawing shows hairs
    barbed or barbellate. Fig. 239.

Barbellate. Finely barbed usually down the sides of
    the structure as well as at the apex.

Basifixed. Attached by the base. Compare versatile.
    Fig. 240.

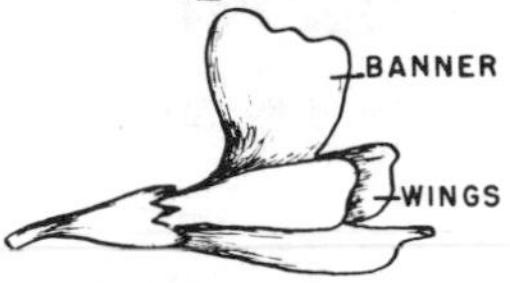

BANNER

WINGS

BANNER OF LEGUME
FLOWER
Fig. 238.

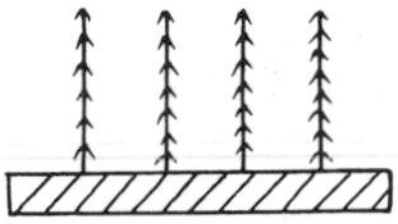

BARBED BRISTLES
Fig. 239.

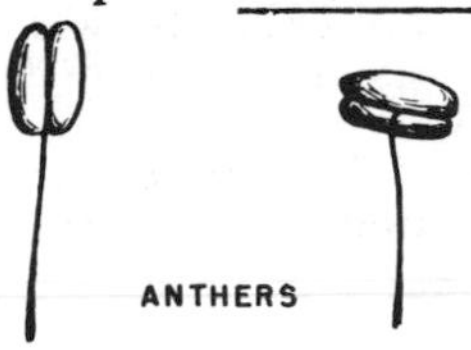

ANTHERS

BASIFIXED
Fig. 240.

VERSATILE

Bast bundle. See vascular
    bundle.

Beak. A hard of firm point or
    projection. Used for the
    ram-like projection on the
    keel of some legume flowers
    or the slender prolongation
    on the fruit of dandelion.
    (Taraxacum). Fig. 241.

BEAK ON KEEL
OF LEGUME
Fig. 241.
No. 1.

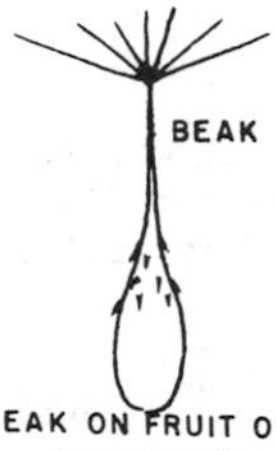

BEAK

BEAK ON FRUIT OF
TARAXACUM
Fig. 241.
No. 2.

Bearded. Furnished with long or stiff
    hairs.

Berry. A fleshy pulpy fruit with im-
    mersed seeds. Rather loosely used.
    The right-hand figure is a longi-
    tudinal section. Fig. 242.

BERRY
Fig. 242.

Bicolored. Of 2 rather sharply contrasting
colors.

Biennial. Living for 2 years.

Bifid. Two-cleft or 2-lobed, usually at the
apex. Fig. 243.

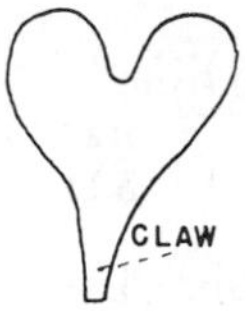

CLAW

BIFID APEX
OF PETAL
Fig. 243.

Bifurcate. Divided into 2 forks or branches.
Fig. 244.

Bilabiate. Two-lipped. Fig. 245.

Bipinnate. Doubly or twice-pinnate, the primary divisions once-again pinnate. Fig. 246.

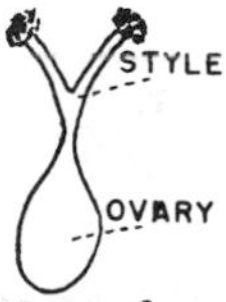

STYLE

OVARY

BIFURCATE
STYLE
Fig. 244.

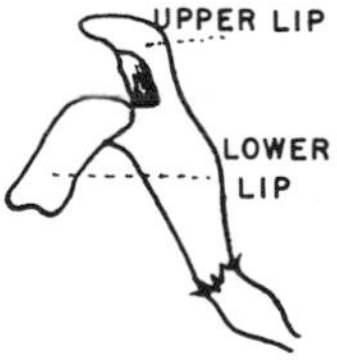

UPPER LIP

LOWER
LIP

BILABIATE COROLLA
Fig. 245.

BIPINNATE LEAF
Fig. 246.

Bisexual. Having both stamens and
pistils, usually used for a flower.
Same as perfect.

Biturbinate. Rather top-shaped but the
widest part not directly at one end.
Fig. 247.

BITURBINATE FRUIT
Fig. 247.

Bladder. An inflated, thin-
walled structure.

Blade. The expanded usually
flat portion of a leaf or
petal. Compare sheath,
petiole and claw. Both a
leaf and a petal are fig-
ured. Fig. 248.

BLADE

PETIOLE

STIPULES

BLADE

BLADE

CLAW

BLADE
Fig. 248.

Bloom. A whitish powdery, glaucous, usually waxy covering of a surface. Also used in reference to a flower.

Bract. A more or less modified leaf situated near a flower or inflorescence. Fig. 249.

BRACTS
Fig. 249.

Bracteate. Having bracts.

Bracteolate. With bractlets.

Bracteole. Same as bractlet.

Bractlet. A secondary bract as one on the pedicel of a flower, usually smaller than the bracts. Also sometimes used for a very small bract. Fig. 250.

BRACTLET
Fig. 250.

Bristle. A stiff hair-like structure on the order of a pig bristle. Fig. 251.

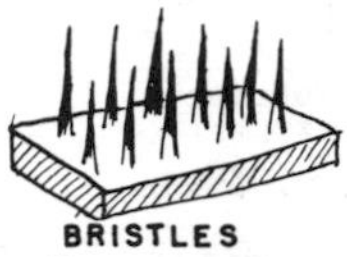

BRISTLES
Fig. 251.

Bud. The rudimentary state of a stem or branch. Also used for an unexpanded flower. Fig. 252.

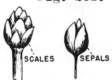

TREE BUD   FLOWER BUD
Fig. 252.

Bulb. A subterranean leaf-bud with fleshy scales like an onion. The drawing is of a bulb in longitudinal section. Fig. 253.

BULB
Fig. 253.

Bulblet. A small bulb especially one borne above the ground as an onion-set.

Bur. A seed or fruit bearing spines or prickles, these usually hooked or barbed. Fig. 254.

BUR
Fig. 254.

Bush. A low thick shrub without a distinct trunk.

Caducous. Falling off unusually early as compared with similar structures in general.

Caespitose. Growing in tufts. Also written cespitose. The illustration shows the base of a plant with many caespitose stems. Fig. 255.

CAESPITOSE
Fig. 255.

Callous. Having a hard texture, often swollen.

Callus. A hard protuberance or callosity. In grasses the indurated downward extension of the lemma, morphologically a part of the rachilla. Fig. 256.

CALLUS TIPPED
LEAF TEETH
Fig. 256.

Calyculate. Having bracts around the calyx or involucre, these usually smaller.

Calyx. The outer series of the perianth, used especially when it differs in size, shape or color from the inner (or petals). Fig. 257.

Calyx tube. That part of the calyx where the sepals are united. Also used for the hypanthium.

Campanulate. Bell-shaped, rather cup-shaped with a flaring rim. Fig. 258.

CALYX-OF
SEPALS
Fig. 257.

CAMPANULATE
COROLLA
Fig. 258.

133

Canaliculate. Longitudinally chan-
neled or grooved. The drawing
shows a fruit cut transversely.
Fig. 259.

CANALICULATE
Fig. 259.

Canescent. With gray or white short
hairs, short-hoary. Often loosely used to mean any gray or white
surface. Fig. 260.

CANESCENT
Fig. 260.

Capillary. Very slender and hair-like.

Capitate. In a globular or head-shaped
cluster. Fig. 261.

CAPITATE
FLOWERS
Fig. 261.

Capitellate. Head-like; a diminutive of capitate.

Capsule. A dry dehiscent fruit made up of more than
1 carpel. Fig. 262.

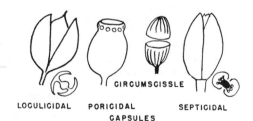

LOCULICIDAL   PORICIDAL   SEPTICIDAL
CAPSULES
CIRCUMSCISSLE

Fig. 262.

Carinate. Keeled with one or more
longitudinal ridges. Fig. 263.

CARINATE FRUIT
Fig. 263.

Carpel. A simple pistil formed from 1
 sporophyll, or that part of a compound pistil formed from 1 sporophyll.
 See figures 47 and 48.

Carpophore. The slender prolongation of
 the floral axis which in Umbelliferae
 supports the pendulous carpels.
 Fig. 264.

CARPOPHORE
Fig. 264.

Cartilaginous. Firm and tough but elastic like
 cartilage.

Caruncle. An excrescence or appendage at or
 about the hilum of a seed. Usually
 fleshy and less tendril-like than an
 aril. Fig. 265.

CARUNCLE
Fig. 265.

Caryopsis. A dry, 1-seeded, indehiscent fruit in
 which the seed is grown fast to the pericarp at
 all points.

Castaneous. Of a chestnut or dark brown color.

Catkin. An ament. Fig. 266.

Caudate. With a slender tail-like appendage.
 Fig. 267.

Caudex (pl. caudices). The persistent, often woody
 base of an otherwise annual herbaceous stem.

Caulescent. Having a manifest leafy stem above
 ground. Compare with acaulescent. Fig. 268.

AMENT-
CATKIN
Fig. 266.

CAUDATE
LEAF TIP
Fig. 267.

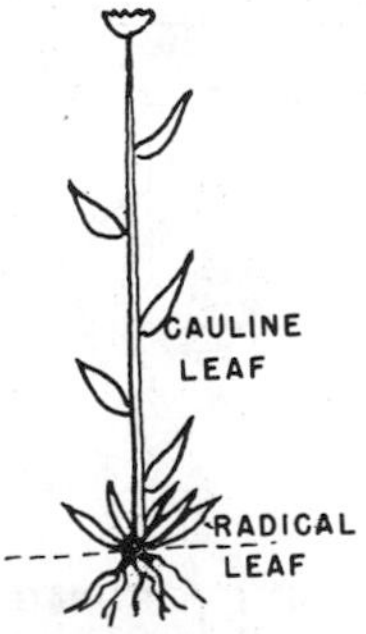

CAULINE
LEAF

RADICAL
LEAF

CAULESCENT PLANT
Fig. 268.

Cauline. Of or pertaining to the stem.

Cauloid. Stem-like.

Cell. A microscopic structural unit of a plant. When used in connection with a pistil then the same as locule.

Cellular. Made up of small pits or compartments.

Centimeter (abbreviation cm.). Ten millimeters or about 2.54 of an inch.

Chaff. A thin dry scale or bract. One of the bracts between the individual flowers in the head of the Compositae.

Chaffy. Possessing or resembling chaff.

Chartaceous. Having the texture of stiff writing paper or parchment.

Chlorophyll. The green pigment associated with photosynthesis.

Ciliate. Beset with a marginal fringe of hairs (cilia). Fig. 269.

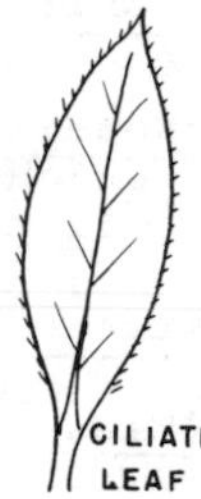

CILIATE LEAF

Fig. 269.

Ciliolate. Ciliate but the hairs minute.

Circinate. Coiled from the tip downward, resembling the upper end of a violin. The figure shows an unfolding fern leaf (or frond). Fig. 270.

Circumscissile. Dehiscing in a transverse circular line, the top separating like the lid of a pill box. Fig. 271.

CIRCINATE FERN FROND

Fig. 270.

CIRCUMSCISSILE CAPSULE

Fig. 271.

Clasping. Describing a sessile leaf with the lower
    edges of the blade partly surrounding the stem.
    Fig. 272.

Clavate. Club-shaped and widest nearer the apex.
    Fig. 273.

Claw. The narrowed base or stalk to some petals.
    The expanded portion would be the blade.
    Fig. 274.

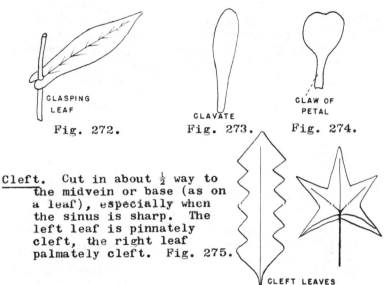

CLASPING
LEAF

CLAVATE

CLAW OF
PETAL

Fig. 272.

Fig. 273.

Fig. 274.

Cleft. Cut in about ½ way to
    the midvein or base (as on
    a leaf), especially when
    the sinus is sharp. The
    left leaf is pinnately
    cleft, the right leaf
    palmately cleft. Fig. 275.

CLEFT LEAVES
Fig. 275.

Cleistogamous. Fertilized in the bud, the flower
    never opening.

Coalescent. Union of parts of the same kind.

Cochleate. Coiled or shaped like a snail shell.

Coerulean. Blue or bluish.

Collateral. Situated at the side of something.

Column. A group of united filaments as in Malvaceae.
    Also the coalesced style and filaments in the
    Orchidaceae.

Coma. A tuft of hairs especially at the
tips of seeds. Fig. 276.

COMA
Fig. 276.

Commissure. The surface by
which 1 carpel joins another
in Umbelliferae. The drawing shows a fruit cut transversely. Fig. 277.

COMISSURAL
SIDE

SEED
RIB

COMMISSURE
Fig. 277.

Comose. Furnished with a
tuft of hairs or coma.

Complete. A flower with
sepals, petals, stamens
and pistils present.

Compound leaf. A leaf completely separated into
2 or more leaflets.
Fig. 278.

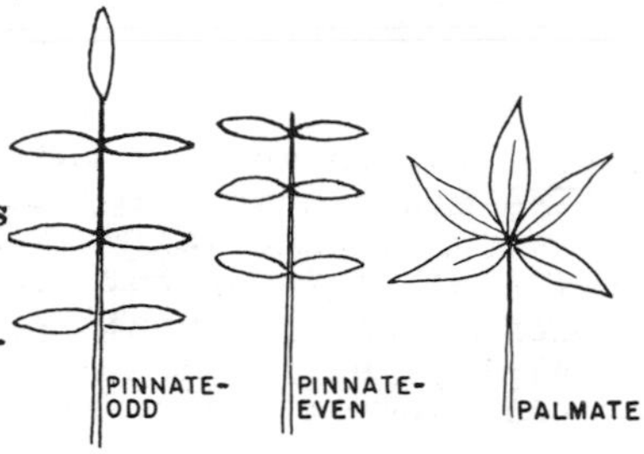

PINNATE-
ODD

PINNATE-
EVEN

PALMATE

COMPOUND LEAVES
Fig. 278.

Compound ovary. An ovary with
2 or more carpels.

Compressed. Flattened especially laterally.

Conduplicate. Folded lengthwise down the middle. The
leaf in the drawing has been
cut transversely.

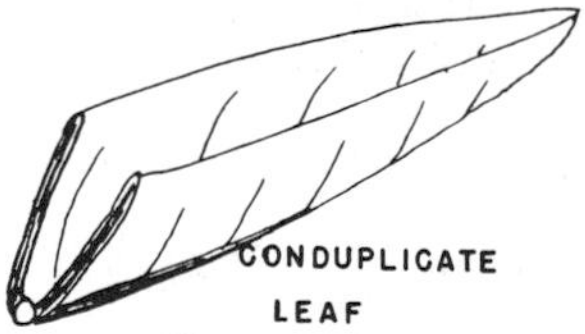

CONDUPLICATE
LEAF
Fig. 279.

138

Cone. The dry multiple fruit of pine,
    spruce etc., consisting of over-
    lapping scales. Same as strobilus.
    Also used as a shape "cone-shaped".
    Fig. 280.

CONE
Fig. 280.

Confluent. Running together; blending in one.

Conical. Cone-shaped, attached at the broad end.

Connate. The union of like structures. Compare
    adnate.

Connective. That portion of a stamen
    that connects the 2 halves of an
    anther. Fig. 281.

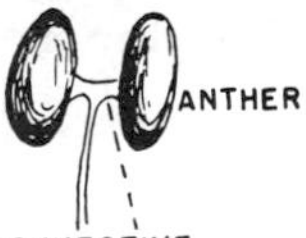

CONNECTIVE
Fig. 281.

Connivent. Converging; in close contact but not
    actually united by tissue.

Continuous. Said of a rachis or axis that does not
    break up at joints at maturity. Compare
    articulate.

Contorted. Twisted or bent or twisted on itself.

Contracted. Said of an inflorescence that is narrow
    and dense with short or appressed branches.

Convolute. Rolled up longitudinally;
    technically one edge inside the
    other but loosely used especially
    in grasses. The drawing shows a
    leaf cut transversely. Fig. 282.

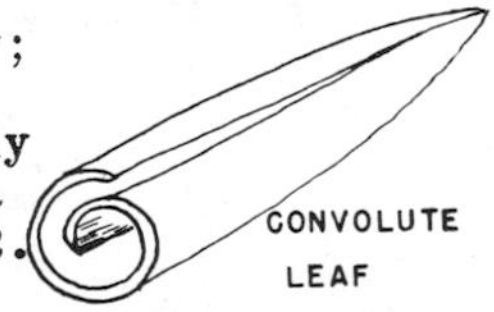

CONVOLUTE
LEAF
Fig. 282.

Cordate. Of a conventional heart shape; the point apical. Compare obcordate. Fig. 283.

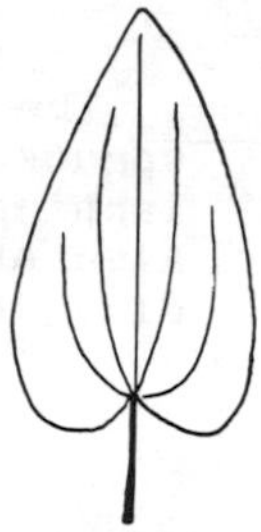

CORDATE LEAF
Fig. 283.

Coriaceous. Texture of leather.

Corm. A thickened, vertical solid underground stem. Compare bulb. The drawing shows a surface view. Fig. 284.

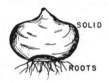

SOLID

ROOTS

CORM
Fig. 284.

Corolla. The inner series of the floral envelope; collective name for petals.

Corona. An appendage or extrusion standing between the corolla and the stamens. Also called a "crown".

Corrugated. Wrinkled or in folds. Fig. 285.

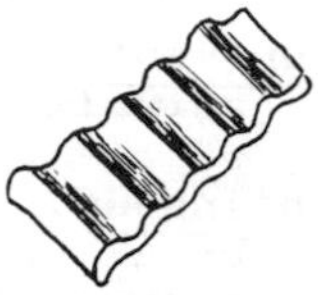

CORRUGATED
Fig. 285.

Cortical. Pertaining to the outer covering.

Corymb. A flat-topped or convex open inflorescence; technically a contracted raceme. Fig. 286.

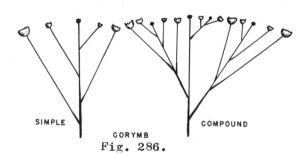

SIMPLE   COMPOUND

CORYMB
Fig. 286.

Corymbiform. Shaped like a corymb.

Corymbose. Borne in corymbs or corymb-like.

Cotyledon. The embryo leaf in a seed,
    often functioning as the first leaf
    of a seedling.

Cremocarp. The dry fruit of the
    Umbelliferae (carrot) family, made
    up of 2 one-seeded mericarps which
    separate at maturity. Also called
    a schizocarp. Fig. 287.

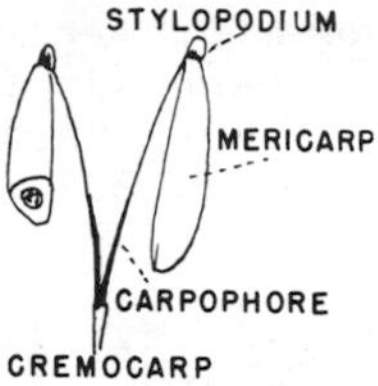

STYLOPODIUM

MERICARP

CARPOPHORE

CREMOCARP

Fig. 287.

Crenate. Toothed with teeth rounded at apex.
    Fig. 288.

Crenulate. Crenate with small teeth.

Crest. An elevated ridge or projection on the sur-
    face.

Crown. An inner appendage to a petal or throat of a
    corolla. Also used for the persistent base of a
    tufted perennial plant especially a grass.
    Fig. 289.

Crustose. Of a hard and brittle texture.

Cucullate. Hooded or hood-shaped; like a cowl.
    Fig. 290.

CRENATE
Fig. 288.

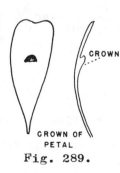

CROWN

CROWN OF
PETAL
Fig. 289.

CUCULLATE PETAL
Fig. 290.

141

Culm. The specialized stem of grasses, sedges and rushes.

Cuneate. Wedge-shaped; rather narrowly triangular, the acute angle downward. Fig. 291.

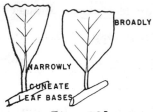

Fig. 291.

Cuspidate. Tipped with an abrupt, short, sharp, firm point. Compare mucronate. Fig. 292.

CUSPIDATE
LEAF TIP
Fig. 292.

Cyathium. The ultimate inflorescence in the genus Euphorbia consisting of unisexual flowers congested within a cup-shaped involucre. Fig. 293.

CYATHIUM OF
EUPHORBIA
Fig. 293.

Cyme. A flower cluster, often convex or flat-topped, in which the central or terminal flower blooms earliest. Fig. 294.

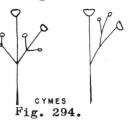

CYMES
Fig. 294.

Cymose. Bearing cymes or cyme-like.

Cymule. A small cyme or portion of one.

Deciduous. Falling away, not persistent or evergreen.

Decompound. More than once-compound, the primary divisions again completely separated.

142

Decumbent. Reclining on the ground but with the end ascending; used for stems. Fig. 295.

DECUMBENT STEM
Fig. 295.

Decurrent. Extending downward from the point of insertion; said of a leaf decurrent on the stem. Fig. 296.

ATTACHED AREA
DECURRENT LEAF
Fig. 296.

Deflexed. Bent or turned abruptly downward or backward. Same as reflexed.

Dehiscent. Opening by definite pores or slits to discharge the contents.

Deliquescent. A type of branching with no well defined central axis running from base to apex.

Deltoid. Shaped like the Greek letter Delta △ , attached at the center of one side. Fig. 297.

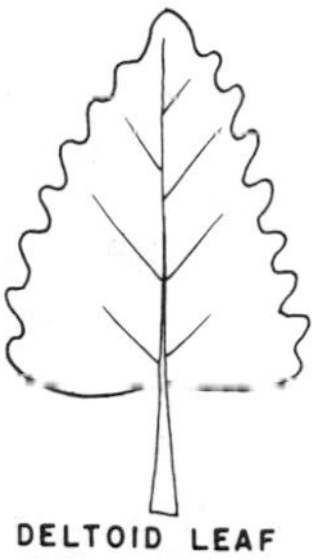

DELTOID LEAF
Fig. 297.

Dense. Said of inflorescences where the flowers are crowded.

Dentate. Toothed with the teeth directed outward. Sometimes loosely used for any large teeth. Fig. 298.

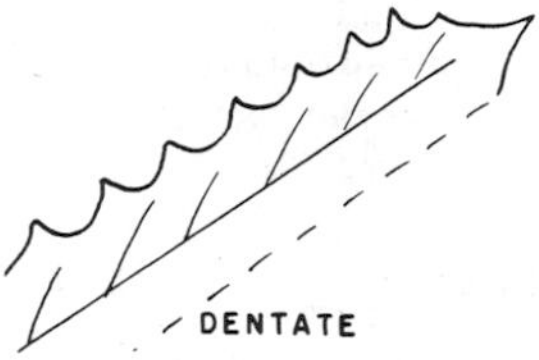

DENTATE
Fig. 298.

Denticles. With minute, usually fragile teeth.

Denticulate. Dentate with small teeth. Fig. 299.

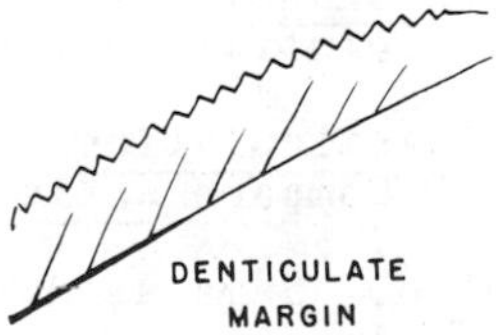

DENTICULATE MARGIN
Fig. 299.

143

Depauperate. Starved or stunted; said of small plants growing under unfavorable conditions.

Depressed. More or less flattened from above.

Diadelphous. Stamens in 2 often unequal sets. Fig. 300.

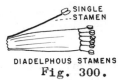
DIADELPHOUS STAMENS
Fig. 300.

Dichotomous. Two-forked, the branches equal or nearly so. Fig. 301.

Didymous. Twin-like; in equal pairs.

Didynamous. Stamens in 2 pairs of unequal length. The drawing shows a two-lipped corolla with 4 stamens protruding beyond the lower lip. Fig. 302.

Diffuse. Loosely or widely spreading.

Digitate. Compound with the parts radiating out from a common point like the fingers on a hand. Same as palmate. Fig. 303.

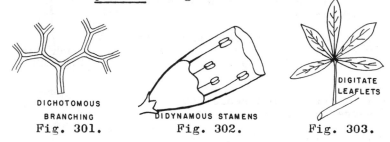

DICHOTOMOUS
BRANCHING
Fig. 301.

DIDYNAMOUS STAMENS
Fig. 302.

DIGITATE
LEAFLETS
Fig. 303.

Dimorphic. In 2 forms.

Dimorphous. With 2 forms.

Dioecious. Flowers unisexual, the staminate and pistillate borne on separate plants.

Disarticulating. The parts separating at maturity. Compare articulating.

Disc. Same as disk.

Discoid. Resembling a disk. A discoid head in Compositae is one where no ray flowers are present.

Disk. An enlargement or prolongation of the receptacle of a flower around the pistil, sometimes made up of coalesced nectaries of staminodia. In the Compositae the central part of the head bearing regular tubular flowers. Fig. 304.

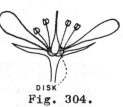

DISK
Fig. 304.

Disk flowers. The regular tubular flowers on the heads of Compositae. Compare ray-flowers or ligules. Fig. 305.

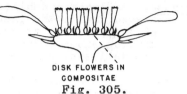

DISK FLOWERS IN COMPOSITAE
Fig. 305.

Dissected. Cut or divided into numerous and usually narrow segments. Too varied to draw.

Distal. The end opposite the point of attachment.

Distichous. In 2 vertical ranks, usually conspicuously so. Fig. 306.

DISTICHOUS LEAVES
Fig. 306.

Distinct. Separate like parts, these not at all united to each other. Compare connate.

Diurnal. Occurring in the daytime.

Divaricate. Widely spreading or diverging.

Divided. Deeply lobed, the sinuses extending to the base of the leaf or to the midrib; nearly compound. Fig. 307.

PINNATE   PALMATE
DIVIDED LEAF MARGINS
Fig. 307.

Dolabriform. Pick-shaped; said of hairs apparently attached at their middle. Fig. 308.

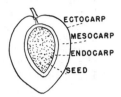

DOLABRIFORM HAIRS

Fig. 308.

Dorsal. Pertaining to the back or outer surface of an organ.

Dorsiventral. On a plane running from the dorsal to the ventral side of a structure. Opposite to lateral.

Drupe. A fleshy indehiscent, 1-seeded fruit, the inner layer of the pericarp stony. The drawing shows a drupe in longitudinal section. Fig. 309.

ECTOCARP
MESOCARP
ENDOCARP
SEED

DRUPE
Fig. 309.

Druplet. A diminutive drupe, as the small parts of a raspberry fruit.

E. A prefix meaning lacking or without.

Eccentric. Not situated at the central axis; off-center.

Echinate. Provided with prickles. Fig. 310.

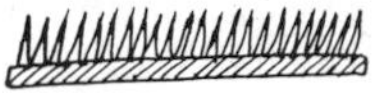

ECHINATE
Fig. 310.

Echinulate. With minute prickles.

Ellipsoid. A solid body, elliptic in outline.

Elliptic. Shaped like an ellipse; widest in center and the 2 ends equal. Loosely used. The drawing shows an average example but the leaf can be longer and narrower and still be elliptic. Fig. 311.

ELLIPTIC LEAF
Fig. 311.

Elliptical. Same as elliptic.

Emarginate. With a shallow notch at the apex.
Fig. 312.

Embryo. The rudimentary plant within a seed.

Endemic. Confined to a limited geographical area.

Endocarp. The inner layer of the pericarp when this
is observable. For an example see drawing of a
drupe.

Endosperm. Substance surrounding the embryo in a
seed.

Ensiform. Shaped like a sword, as the leaf of Iris.
Fig. 313.

Entire. Margins without teeth or lobes. Fig. 314.

EMARGINATE
APEX
Fig. 312.

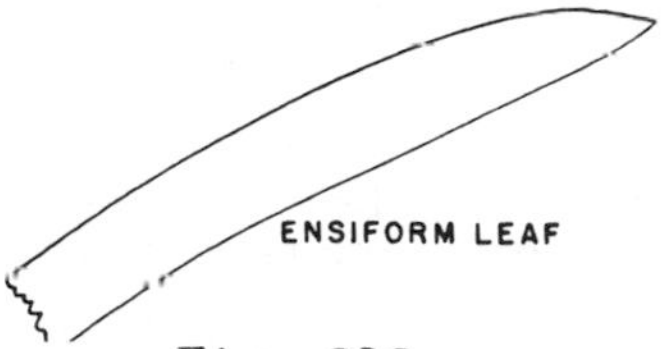

ENSIFORM LEAF

Fig. 313.

ENTIRE MARGIN
Fig. 314.

Entomophilous. Pollinated by insects.

Ephemeral. Lasting for one day or less.

Epidermis. The outer layer of cells.

Epigynous. Growing on the summit of
the ovary or appearing to do so.
The drawing shows a flower in
longitudinal section. Fig. 315.

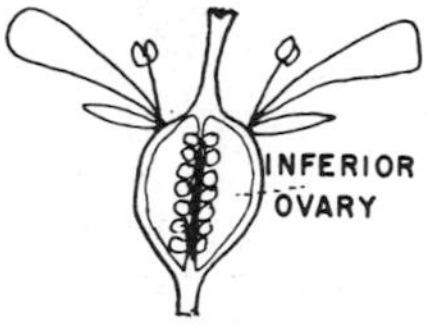

INFERIOR
OVARY

EPIGYNOUS
FLOWER
Fig. 315.

Equitant. Leaves that are conduplicate and in 2 ranks; also 2-ranked leaves, flattened with edges toward and away from the axis. Fig. 316.

Erose. Margin irregular as if gnawed. Fig. 317.

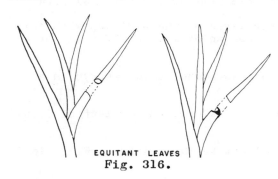

EQUITANT LEAVES
Fig. 316.

EROSE
Fig. 317.

Erosulate. More of less erose.

Even-pinnate. A pinnately compound leaf ending in a pair of leaflets, hence presumably with an even number of leaflets. Fig. 318.

Evergreen. Bearing green leaves throughout the year. Compare deciduous.

Ex. A prefix meaning lacking or without.

EVEN
PINNATE
LEAF
Fig. 318.

Excurrent. Running out or beyond, as a nerve of a leaf projecting out beyond the margin. Also used for habit of a tree where there is one main unbranched axis from bottom to top as in a spruce or fir tree. Fig. 319. and Fig. 320.

Excurved. Curving outward or away from the axis.

Exfoliating. Peeling off in thin layers.

EXCURRENT
LEAF TIP
Fig. 319.

EXCURRENT
BRANCHING
Fig. 320.

148

Exocarp. The outer layer of the pericarp. For an example see the drawing of a drupe.

Exotic. Not native, introduced from another area. Compare indigenous.

Explanate. Spread out flat.

Exserted. Projecting beyond a surrounding organ, as a stamen exserted from a corolla. Compare included. Fig. 321.

EXSERTED
STAMENS

Fig. 321.

Extrorse. Facing outward, often used for anthers turned away from the center of the flower.

Falcate. Scythe- or scimiter-shaped, curved sidewise and flat, tapering upwards; asymmetric. Fig. 322.

FALCATE LEAF

Fig. 322.

Fan-shaped. Shaped like an opened folding fan; triangular with the upper side convex. Fig. 323.

Farinaceous. Starchy; mealy.

Farinose. Covering with a mealy usually whitish substance.

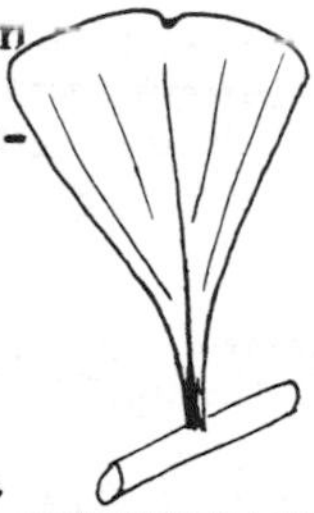

FAN SHAPED LEAF

Fig. 323.

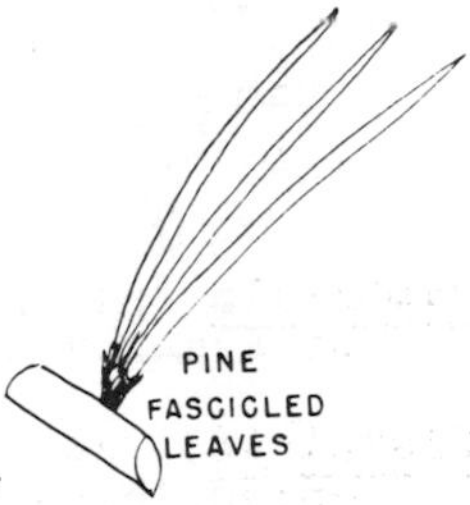

PINE
FASCICLED
LEAVES

Fig. 324.

Fascicled. Borne in close bundles or clusters. Fig. 324.

Fastigiate. Erect or near together with a broom-like effect.

Fern-like. Used of a leaf dissected or divided into narrow segments like many ferns.

149

Fertile. Capable of producing fruit and seeds; a
      fertile flower may be pistillate or perfect.

Fetid. With a disagreeable odor.

Fibrillose. With fine fibers. Sometimes written
      fibrillate.

Fibrous. Composed of, or resembling
      fibers.

Filament. Any thread-like body; used es-
      pecially for that part of the stamen
      that supports the anther. Fig. 325.

FILAMENT
OF STAMEN
Fig. 325.

Filamentose. Composed of threads. Also
      written filamentous.

Filiferous. Producing or bearing thread-
      like growths.

Filiform. Thread-like; long, slender
      and terete.

Fimbriate. Margins with a fringe of
      hairs, these longer and coarser
      than ciliate. Fig. 326.

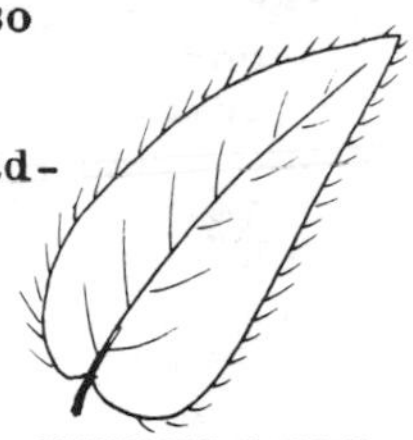

FIMBRIATE MARGIN
Fig. 326.

Fimbrilla (pl. fimbrillae). A single unit
      of a marginal fringe.

Fistulose. Hollow and cylindrical like
      onion leaves, often rather enlarged.
      Also written fistulous. Fig. 327.

FISTULOSE
STEM
Fig. 327

Flabellate. Same as fan-shaped.

Flabelliform. Same as fan-shaped.

Flaccid. Lax and weak; without rigidity.

150

Flange. A projecting edge or rim; edge
flaring and conspicuous. Fig. 328.

Fig. 328.

Flexuose. Same as flexuous.

Flexuous. Bent alternately in opposite directions,
usually not strongly so. Fig. 329.

Floccose. Clothed with loose tufts of wool-like
hair, this not uniform over the entire surface.
Fig. 330.

Floral envelope. The collective name for the sepals
and petals. Same as perianth.

Floret. A small flower especially one in a dense
cluster. Also a special term for a grass flower
with its lemma and palea included.

Floricane. The flowering and fruiting cane (stem)
of a bramble (genus Rubus).

Floriferous. Bearing flowers.

Fluted. With grooves or furrows. Fig. 331.

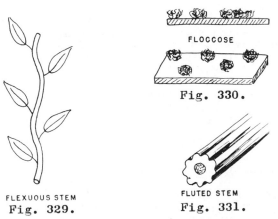

FLOCCOSE

Fig. 330.

FLEXUOUS STEM
Fig. 329.

FLUTED STEM
Fig. 331.

Foliaceous. Leaf-like especially in color.

151

-foliate. Having leaves.

-foliolate. Having leaflets.

Follicle. A dry fruit with 1 carpel and splitting
  down one side only. Fig. 332.

Fornix (pl. fornices). Small arching crests in the
  throat of a corolla. The illustration shows the
  corolla tube split and flattened out. Fig. 333.

Fovea. (pl. foveae). Small depressions or pits.
  Fig. 334.

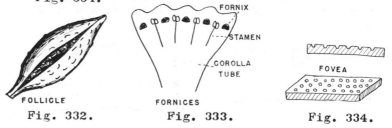

FOLLICLE   FORNICES

Fig. 332.   Fig. 333.   Fig. 334.

Free. Not adnate; unlike parts not connected.

Free central placenta. The ovary is one-celled and
  the ovules are borne on a central stalk not connected at the top. Both a longitudinal and
  cross-section are figured. Fig. 335.

Frond. Leaf of a fern. In Lemnaceae the expanded
  thallus-like stem which functions as a leaf.
  Fern leaves are usually more dissected or decompound than in the one illustrated. (See
  Fig. 102 also). Fig. 336.

Fruit. The ripened ovary and
  any other structures that
  enclose it at maturity.

Fruticose. Shrub-like; at
  least somewhat woody.
  Also written frutescent.

Fugacious. Falling or fading very early. About
  the same as caducous.

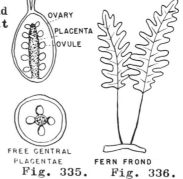

FREE CENTRAL
PLACENTAE   FERN FROND
Fig. 335.   Fig. 336.

152

Fulvous. Dull yellow; yellow tinged with brown or gray.

Funiculus (pl. funiculi). The ovule stem or attachment structure. The ovary is shown in longitudinal section. Fig. 337.

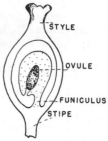

Fig. 337.

Funnelform. With the tube widening upward passing gradually into the limb. Fig. 338.

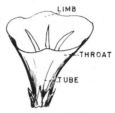

Fig. 338.

Furfuraceous. Resembling flakes or grains of bran; scurfy.

Fuscous. Grayish-brown or dusky-brown.

Fusiform. Spindle-shaped; broadest at the middle and tapering both ways. Fig. 339.

FUSIFORM

Fig. 339.

Galea. A hooded or helmet-shaped part of the perianth, usually the upper lip of an irregular corolla. Fig. 340.

Galeate. Shaped like a galea or helmet.

Gametophyte. The sexual stage in plants which bear sperm and eggs. Used particularly for the prothallus of ferns.

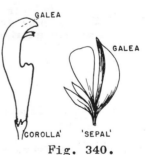

Fig. 340.

Gamopetalous. Petals more or less united. Same as sympetalous.

153

Gamophyllous. The leaves or leaf-like organs more or less united one to another.

Gamosepalous. The sepals more or less united.

Geminate. Equal, in pairs like twins.

Gemma (pl. gemmae). A bud or bud-like body by which some plants propagate themselves.

Geniculate. Bent abruptly like knee or stove pipe bend. Fig. 341.

Gibbous. Enlarged, humped or swollen on one side. Fig. 341. Fig. 342.

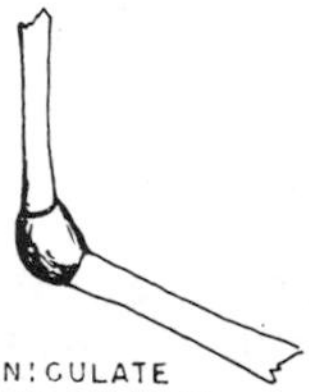

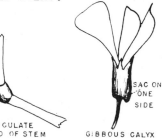

GENICULATE
BEND OF STEM

SAC ON ONE SIDE

GIBBOUS CALYX
Fig. 342.

Glabrate. Becoming glabrous in age.

Glabrescent. About the same as glabrate.

Glabrous. No hairs present at all; also used for smooth.

Gland. A secreting surface or structure, or an appendage having the general appearance of such an organ.

Glandular. Bearing glands. A glandular hair has an enlargement like a hat pin at the apex. Fig. 343.

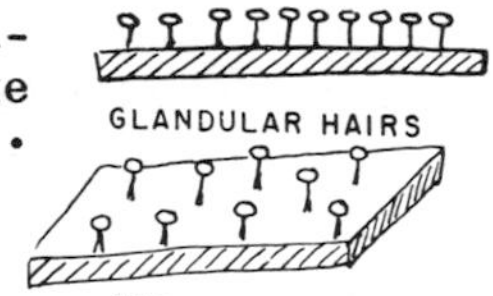

GLANDULAR HAIRS

Fig. 343.

Glaucescent. Tending to be glaucous; somewhat glaucous.

Glaucous. Covered with a whitish or bluish waxy covering; this should readily rub off but the term is sometimes loosely used for any whitish surface.

Globose. Shaped like a globe,
like a model of the earth.
The drawing shows the two
halves. Fig. 344.

GLOBOSE   GLOCHIDS
Fig. 344. Fig. 345

Glochid. A barbed hair or bristle;
usually used for the minute
bristles in Opuntia. Fig. 345.

Glochidiate. Barbed at the tip.

Glomerate. Crowded, congested or compactly clustered.

Glomerule. A dense crowded cluster, usually of
flowers.

Glume. A chaff-like bract; used particularly for the
2 lower empty bracts of a grass spikelet.

Glutinous. Covered with a sticky
glue-like or gummy exudation.

Grain. A swollen, seed-like structure
as on the fruit of some species
of Rumex; also used as a synonym
for caryopsis. Fig. 346.

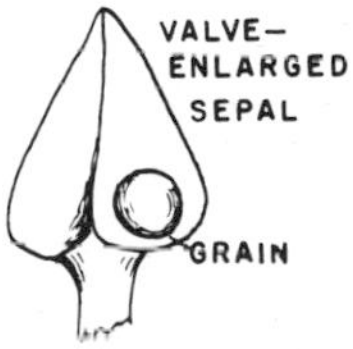

VALVE-
ENLARGED
SEPAL

GRAIN

RUMEX FRUIT
Fig. 346.

Granulate. Composed of, or appearing to be covered
by small granules. Same as granulose.

Granule. A minute rounded object.

Granuliferous. Composed of, or covered with very
minute granules.

Grass-like. Resembling grasses; usually used for
sedges and rushes.

Grenadin. A conspicuous orange- or brick-red color
most characteristic of the petals of Sphaeralcea.

155

Gynobase. An enlargement or prolongation
of the receptacle bearing the ovary.
The flower in the drawing has been cut
in half longitudinally with only two
of the four nutlets showing. Fig.
347.

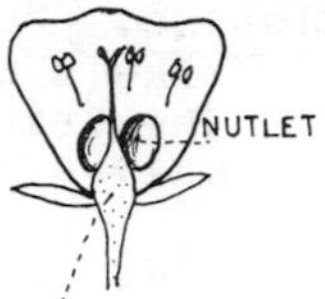

GYNOBASE IN
BORAGINACEAE
Fig. 347.

Gynoecium. A collective name for the
pistils.

Halberd-shaped. Same as hastate.

Hastate. Arrow-head shaped but with the
basal lobes pointing outward instead
of backward. Used either for a shape   HASTATE LEAF
or to describe the base alone. Fig.   Fig. 348.
348.

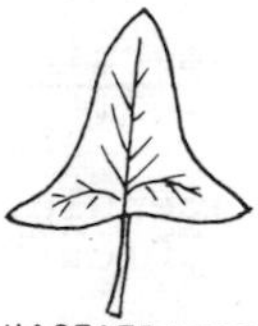

Haustoria. Root-like sucking attachments of parasitic plants like Cuscuta (dodder).

Head. A dense cluster of sessile or nearly sessile
flowers or fruits on a very short axis; used
especially for the involucrate inflorescence in
Compositae.

Herb. A plant with no persistent woody stem above
ground; also a plant used in seasoning and medi-
cine.

Herbaceous. Having the characteristic of a herb;
also leaf-like in color or texture.

Hermaphroditic. A flower with both stamens and
pistils. Same as perfect and bisexual.

Heteromorphous. Of more than 1 kind or form.

Heterostyled. With more than 1 length of
style.

Hilum. The scar or point of attachment
of a seed. Fig. 349.

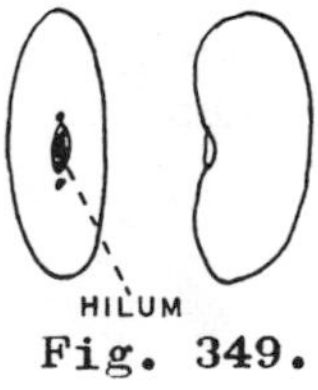

HILUM
Fig. 349.

Hirsute. With moderately coarse and stiff hairs. Fig. 350.

Hirsutulose. Same as hirsutulous.

Hirsutulous. Somewhat hirsute.

Hirtellous. Minutely hirsute.

Hispid. With stiff and rigid bristles or bristle-like hairs, these usually stiff enough to penetrate the skin. Fig. 351.

Hispidulous. Minutely hispid.

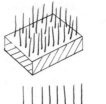

HIRSUTE

Fig. 350.

HISPID

Fig. 351.

HOOKED APEX OF FRUIT

Fig. 352.

HORNED FRUIT

Fig. 353.

Hoary. Covered with white or gray short fine hairs.

Homomorphous. Of only 1 form or kind.

Hooked. Abruptly curved at tip. Fig. 352.

Horn. A stiff tapering appendage somewhat like the horn of a cow. Fig. 353.

Hyaline. Thin, dry and transparent or translucent.

Hydrophyte. A plant that grows in water. Compare mesophyte and xerophyte.

Hygroscopic. Altering form or position due to changes in moisture content.

Hypanthium. An enlargement or elongation of the floral axis below the calyx, commonly partly or completely enclosing the pistils; when this occurs the ovary is here considered to be inferior. Fig. 354.

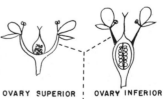

OVARY SUPERIOR OVARY INFERIOR

HYPANTHIUM

Fig. 354.

157

Hypogynous. Situated on the receptacle
    below the ovary; a flower having
    the petals and stamens so situated.
    Fig. 355.

HYPOGYNOUS
Fig. 355.

Imbricate. Partly overlapping like
    shingles on a roof, either ver-
    tically or laterally. The draw-
    ing to the right shows a cross-
    section of lateral imbrication.
    Fig. 356.

IMBRICATE
Fig. 356.

Immersed. Growing submerged in water.

Imperfect flowers. Lacking either stamens or
    pistils. Compare perfect, unisexual and bi-
    sexual.

Incised. Cut sharply and us-
    ually irregularly with
    sharp sinuses, deeper than
    teeth but seldom as deep as
    ½ way in to the base or
    midrib. The leaf at the
    left is pinnately incised,
    the one at the right is
    palmately so. Fig. 357.

INCISED LEAF
MARGINS

Fig. 357.

Included. Not at all protruding
    from the surrounding organ.
    The right figure shows a
    corolla split down one side
    and rolled flat. Fig. 358.

INCLUDED STAMENS
Fig. 358.

Incurved. Curved toward the axis or attachment.

Indehiscent. Remaining persistently closed; not
    opening by definite lines or pores.

Indigenous. Native to the area. Compare exotic.

Indurated. Hardened and stiffened.

Indusium (pl. indusia). The thin scale-like out-
    growth of the fern leaf forming a covering for
    the young sorus. Sometimes the inrolled margin
    functions as an indusium.

Inferior ovary. One that is adnate to
    the hypanthium or calyx tube, ap-
    pearing to be sunken in the stem, the
    flower parts appearing to come off
    from above the ovary; used here in
    the broad sense. Fig. 359.

INFERIOR OVARY
Fig. 359.

Inflated. Bladder-like; enlarged with
    thin walls. Fig. 360.

INFLATED POD
Fig. 360.

Inflexed. Turned abruptly or bent inwards; incurved.

Inflorescence. The flowering part of a plant, almost
    always used for a flower cluster.

Infrastipular. Situated below the stipules; used in
    Rosa when a pair of prickles below the node is
    enlarged or conspicuous because of the absence
    or scarcity of other prickles. Fig. 361.

Innovation. A basal offshoot from the main stem,
    shorter and less modified than a rhizome or
    stolon; in grasses an incomplete young shoot.
    Fig. 362.

INFRASTIPULAR
PRICKLES
Fig. 361.

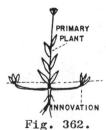

PRIMARY
PLANT

INNOVATION
Fig. 362.

Internode. The portion of a stem or other structure between 2 nodes. Fig. 363.

Interrupted. Not continuous. Usually used for pinnately compound leaves where small leaflets are interspersed among the larger ones. Fig. 364.

Introduced. A plant brought in intentionally from another area, as for purposes of cultivation. Such a plant may later escape and persist.

Introrse. Turned in or facing inward, as an anther turned in toward the center of a flower. Fig. 365.

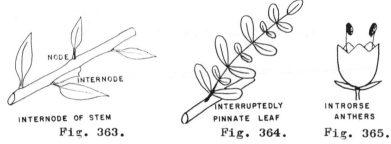

INTERNODE OF STEM
Fig. 363.

INTERRUPTEDLY PINNATE LEAF
Fig. 364.

INTRORSE ANTHERS
Fig. 365.

Involucel. A secondary involucre as in Umbelliferae. Fig. 366.

Involucrate. With an involucre.

Involucre. A whorl of distinct or united leaves or bracts subtending a flower or an inflorescence. Fig. 367.

Involute. Both edges inrolled toward the midnerve on the upper surface; loosely used in grasses for any leaf rolled on the upper surface. Compare revolute. Fig. 368.

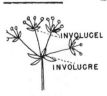

INVOLUCEL
Fig. 366.

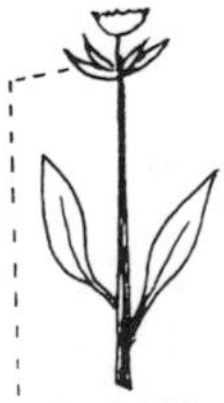

INVOLUCRE
Fig. 367.

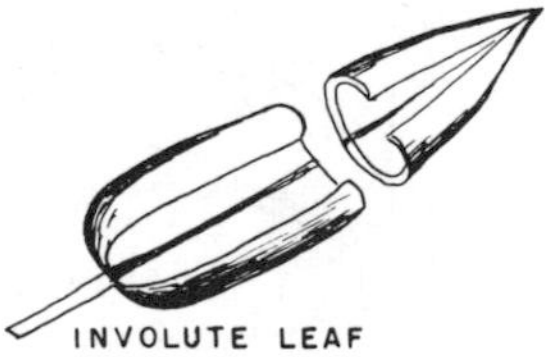

INVOLUTE LEAF
Fig. 368.

160

Irregular flower. With inequality in the size, form
    or union of its similar parts; not radially sym-
    metrical. Same as zygomorphic. Fig. 369.

Keel. A dorsal projecting usually central rib, like
    the keel of a boat; also the name for the 2
    anterior united petals of a papilionaceous
    "sweetpea" flower as figured on the right-hand
    drawing. Fig. 370.

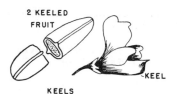

IRREGULAR FLOWERS
Fig. 369.

KEELS
Fig. 370.

Labiate. Lipped. Belonging to the Labiatae or mint
    family.

Lacerate. Irregularly cut or cleft, as if torn.

Laciniate. Narrowly incised or slashed; margins cut
    in narrow and usually pointed lobes. Fig. 371.

Lacuna (pl. lacunae). An air space in the midst of
    tissue.

Lamella (pl. lamellae). A thin flat plate or later-
    ally flattened ridge. The drawing shows a fruit
    in longitudinal section. Fig. 372.

Lanate. With long tangled woolly hairs. Fig. 373.

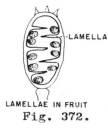

LACINIATE
LEAF MARGINS
Fig. 371.

LAMELLAE IN FRUIT
Fig. 372.

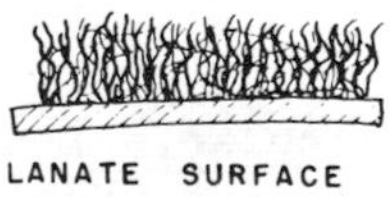

LANATE SURFACE
Fig. 373.

161

Lanceolate. Lance-shaped; several
    times longer than wide, broadest
    toward the base and tapering to
    apex. Fig. 374.

LANCEOLATE
LEAF

Fig. 374.

Lateral. Borne on the sides of a structure or ob-
    ject.

Latex. The milky juice of some plants like milkweed
    and dandelion.

Lax. Loose; often used for a soft open inflorescence
    or for soft drooping stems or foliage.

Leaflet. One of the divisions of a compound leaf.

Legume. The characteristic fruit of
    the Leguminosae family; usually
    a dehiscent fruit formed from 1
    carpel with 2 lines of dehiscence.
    Also used for any plant with this
    type of fruit. Fig. 375.

LEGUME
FRUIT

Fig. 375.

Lenticel. A group of loose corky cells
    formed beneath the epidermis of
    woody plants, rupturing the epider-
    mis and admitting gases to and from
    the inner tissues. Fig. 376.

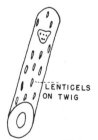

LENTICELS
ON TWIG

Fig. 376.

Lenticular. Lens-shaped; biconvex in shape
    In the drawing the object is cut into 2
    parts. Fig. 377.

LENTICULAR
Fig. 377.

162

Lepidote. Covered with small scurfy scales like
the leaf of Elaeagnus (Russian Olive).

Ligulate. Furnished with a ligule; also used for a
strap shape like a ligule.

Ligule. The flattened, usually strap-shaped corolla
in the ray flowers of Compositae. Also a hair-
like or membranous projection up from the inside
of a grass sheath at its junction with the blade.
Fig. 378.

Limb. The expanded portion of a gamopetalous corolla
above the throat; the expanded portion of any
organ. Fig. 379.

Linear. Narrow and flat with sides parallel, like a
grass leaf blade. Fig. 380.

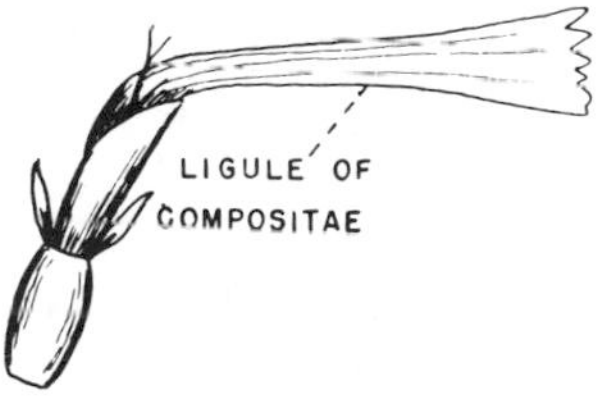

LIGULE OF
COMPOSITAE

THROAT

TUBE

LIMB OF COROLLA

LINEAR
LEAF

Fig. 378. 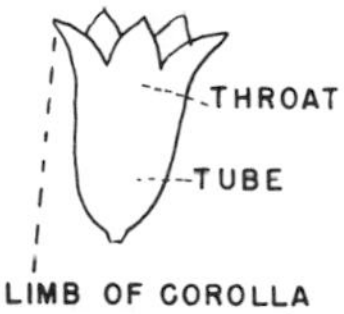   Fig. 379. 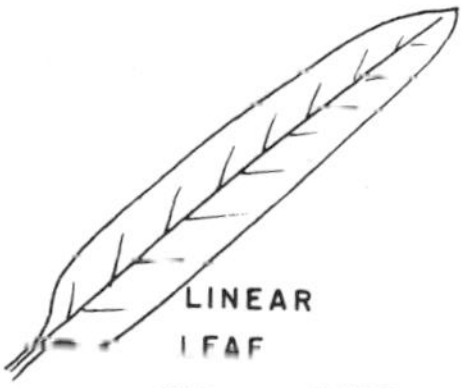   Fig. 380.

Lip. Either the upper or lower division of a bilabiate or 2-lipped corolla. Also the upper (but
by twisting of the pedicel appearing to be the
lower) petal in Orchidaceae.

Lobe. Any segment of an organ especially if rounded.

Lobed. Bearing lobes; loosely
used but technically cut in
not over half way to the base
or midvein, the sinuses and
apex of segments rounded.
The left figure shows a pinnately lobed leaf, the right
a palmately lobed one.
Fig. 381.

LOBED LEAVES
Fig. 381.

163

Lobulate. With small lobes.

Locule. The cell or compartment of
an ovary or anther.

Loculicidal. A dehiscent fruit
splitting down the center of a
compartment or locule. Fig. 382.

LOCULICIDAL
FRUIT

Fig. 382.

Loment. A legume fruit conspicuously constricted between
the seeds. Fig. 383.

Lunate. Crescent-shaped like
the crescent moon. Fig.
384.

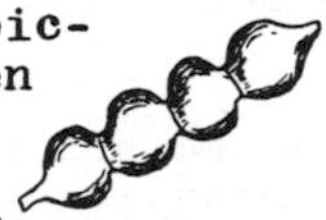

LOMENT FRUIT
Fig. 383.

LUNATE
Fig. 384.

Lyrate. Pinnatifid with the terminal
segment large and rounded and the
lower lobes small. Fig. 385.

LYRATE LEAF

Fig. 385.

Macrospore. Same as megaspore.

Malpighiaceous. Straight hairs seemingly attached
by their middle, pick-shaped. Same as
dolabriform, see this for sketches.

Many. Eleven or more. Same as numerous.

Marcescent. Withering but still persistent.

Mealy. A surface covered with minute particles
these usually rounded.

Medial. Refers to the middle of a structure.

Megasporangium. (pl. megasporangia). The containing
structure for the large spores or megaspores.

Megaspore. The larger of the two kinds of spores,
used particularly in the Pteridophytes.

164

Membranaceous. Same as membranous.

Membranous. Thin, more or less translucent and
pliable; loosely used in grasses for any thin
structure.

Mericarp. A portion of a fruit that splits
away as a seemingly separate unit, most
commonly used for the two halves of the
fruit of Umbelliferae. Fig. 386.

MERICARP

Fig. 386.

Meristem. Tissue with cells not as yet differentiated, often exhibiting active cell division.

-merous. A suffix indicating division into parts.
A "5-merous flower" would have 5 sepals, 5
petals, 5 stamens and a 5 carpellate pistil
(providing all these structures were present).

Mesocarp. The middle layer of the pericarp. For an
example see figure for drupe.

Mesophyte. A plant that grows under medium or
average conditions especially of moisture supply. Compare hydrophyte and xerophyte.

Meter. (Abbreviation M. or m.). Unit of measurement
consisting of 100 centimeters; almost 40 inches.

Micron. A microscopic unit of measurement, 1/1000
of a millimeter.

Microsporangium (pl. microsporangia). The containing
structure for the small spores or microspores.

Microspore. The smaller kind of spore when
2 types are present; used especially in
the Pteridophytes.

Midrib. The main or central rib of a leaf.
Fig. 387.

MIDRIB

Fig. 387.

Millimeter. (Abbreviation mm.).
‾‾‾‾‾A small unit of measurement,
1/10 of a centimeter or
about 1/25 of an inch.

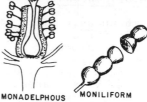

Monadelphous. Stamens united
‾‾‾‾‾by their filaments into one
set. Fig. 388.

Moniliform. Cylindrical with
‾‾‾‾‾rounded contractions at regular intervals, resembling a
string of beads. Fig. 389.

MONADELPHOUS   MONILIFORM
STAMENS   FRUIT
Fig. 388. Fig. 389.

Monoecious. Flowers unisexual but the staminate and
‾‾‾‾‾pistillate ones borne on the same plant.

Monophyllous. Used for leaves in plants where re-
‾‾‾‾‾lated species have compound leaves, but the
leaflets here reduced to one.

Monotypic. When refering to a genus, then one with
‾‾‾‾‾only a single species in it.

Moss-like. With low thin stems and small thin
‾‾‾‾‾leaves like a moss plant.

Mucilaginous. Slimy or mucilage-like.

Mucro. A short, small, abrupt tooth-like
‾‾‾‾‾tip; loosely used but not very sharp
at extreme apex. Compare cuspidate.
Fig. 390.

MUCRO
ON LEAF TIP
Fig. 390.

Mucronate. Tipped with a mucro.

Mucronulate. Minutely mucronate, the mucro very
‾‾‾‾‾small.

Multicellular. Consisting of many cells or small
‾‾‾‾‾compartments.

Multicipital. With many heads, referring to the
‾‾‾‾‾crown of a single root or to several caudices.

Multifid. Cleft into many lobes or segments, these
‾‾‾‾‾usually narrow.

166

Multiple fruit. One formed from several flowers crowded into a single unit on a common axis, as in the mulberry.

Muricate. Roughened with short hard points. Fig. 391.

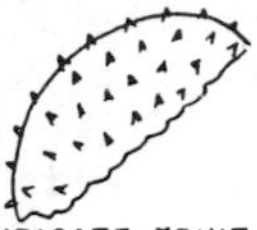

MURICATE FRUIT

Fig. 391.

Muriculate. Very finely muricate.

Muticous. Blunt and without a point.

Naked. Lacking some structure, appendage or hairs which might ordinarily be expected to be present.

Nectary. A gland or tissue for secreting nectar; often located in highly specialized structures which may themselves be called "nectaries".

Needle-like. Long, slender, rather rigid and more or less sharp at apex like a needle. Usually round or square in cross-section but sometimes flattened. See acerose for drawings.

Nerve. A simple or unbranched vein or slender rib.

Nerviform. On the order of a nerve.

Netted. Same as reticulated.

Net-veined. The veins joining together on the order of a fish net.

Neuter. Without functional stamens or pistils. Same as neutral.

Neutral. See neuter.

Node. The place on a stem where leaves or branches normally originate; the place on an axis that bears other structures; any swollen or knob-like structure. See internode for a figure.

Nodose. Knobby or knotty.

Nodulose. Provided with minute knobs.

Numerous. Eleven or more. Same as many.

Nut. A 1-seeded, indehiscent fruit with a hard wall.

Nutlet. A small nut or nut-
like fruit; used es-
pecially for the sepa-
rating lobes of the
mature ovary in
Boraginaceae, Labiatae
and Verbenaceae. The
drawing shows 2 of the
4 nutlets. Fig. 392.

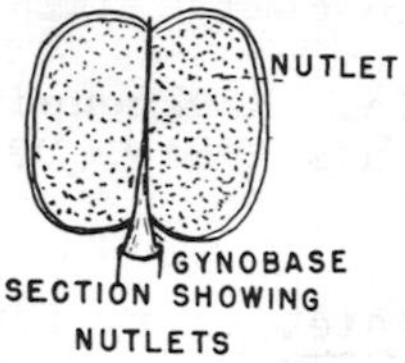

NUTLET

GYNOBASE
SECTION SHOWING
NUTLETS

Fig. 392.

Ob-. A prefix signifying inversion.

Obcompressed. Flattened opposite to the usual way,
for example flattened dorso-ventrally instead
of laterally.

Obconical. Inversely cone-shaped, attached at the pointed end. The drawing shows a 3-dimensional figure.
Fig. 393.

OBCONICAL

Fig. 393.

Obcordate. Inverted heart-shaped, attached at the
point. Also used in reference to a deeply notch-
ed apex irrespective of the general leaf shape.
Fig. 394.

Oblanceolate. Inversely lanceolate, attached at the
tapered end. Fig. 395.

Oblique. Sides unequal, especially the base of a
leaf. Fig. 396.

OBCORDATE LEAF
Fig. 394.

OBLANCEOLATE
LEAF
Fig. 395.

OBLIQUE BASE
Fig. 396.

Oblong. Two to four times longer than wide and the sides parallel or nearly so. Fig. 397.

Obovate. Inversely ovate, attached at the narrow end. Fig. 398.

Obovoid. A 3-dimensional figure of obovate outline.

Obsolete. Rudimentary or not at all evident; particularly applied to organs usually present.

Obtuse. Blunt or rounded at the apex. Fig. 399.

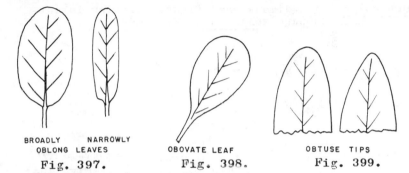

BROADLY   NARROWLY
OBLONG LEAVES
Fig. 397.

OBOVATE LEAF
Fig. 398.

OBTUSE TIPS
Fig. 399.

Ochroleucous. Yellowish-white or cream-colored.

Ocrea (pl. ocreae). A tubular stipule or pair of sheathing confluent elongated stipules. Characteristic in the family Polygonaceae. Fig. 400.

Odd-pinnate. A pinnately compound leaf with a single terminal leaflet. Fig. 401.

OCREA
Fig. 400.

ODD-PINNATE LEAF
Fig. 401.

169

Oil tube. Small longitudinal ducts in the walls of the fruit of Umbelliferae presumably containing volatile oils. Fig. 402.

Oogonium (pl. oogonia). The container for the oospore.

Oospore. The egg cell with a somewhat hardened outer coat.

Opposite. Leaves 2 at a node and situated across the stem from each other. Fig. 403.

Orbicular. A 2-dimensional figure circular in out-line. Compare spherical. Fig. 404.

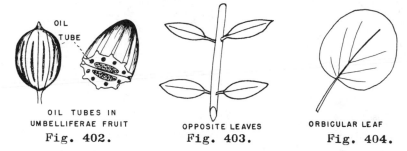

OIL
TUBE

OIL TUBES IN
UMBELLIFERAE FRUIT
Fig. 402.

OPPOSITE LEAVES
Fig. 403.

ORBICULAR LEAF
Fig. 404.

Oval. Loosely used for broadly elliptical, the width over ½ the length; some authors have used it as the same as ovate. Fig. 405.

Ovary. That part of the pistil that contains the ovules. The ovary is shown in longitudinal section. Fig. 406.

Ovate. Egg-shaped in outline, attached at the wide end. Fig. 407.

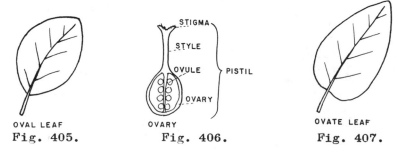

STIGMA

STYLE

OVULE

PISTIL

OVARY

OVAL LEAF
Fig. 405.

OVARY
Fig. 406.

OVATE LEAF
Fig. 407.

170

Ovoid. A 3-dimensional figure, ovate in outline.

Ovule. The structure that develops into the seed.
The ovary is shown in longitudinal section.
Fig. 408.

Palate. A rounded projection on the lower lip of a
bilabiate corolla, closing the throat. Fig.
409.

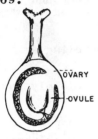

OVULE
Fig. 408.

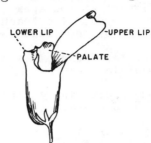

PALATE ON PERSONATE COROLLA
Fig. 409.

Palea (pl. paleae or paleas). A chaffy scale or
bract; the inner of the 2 bracts enclosing the
grass flower. Compare lemma.

Paleaceous. Chaffy, thin, small and often translucent.

Palmate. The lobes or divisions attached or running
down toward one place at the base. Compare
pinnate. Also used to describe the veins of certain leaves. Fig. 410 and Fig. 411.

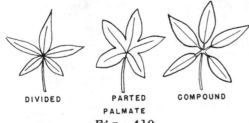

DIVIDED   PARTED   COMPOUND
PALMATE
Fig. 410.

PALMATELY VEINED
Fig. 411.

Palustrine. Inhabiting wet ground, marsh dwelling.

Pandurate. Fiddle-shaped. Same as panduriform. Fig. 412.

Panduriform. Same as pandurate.

Panicle. A compound inflorescence with the younger flowers at the apex or center; a compound raceme or corymb. The "rachis" may be called the "main axis" by some manuals. Fig. 413.

Paniculate. Borne in a panicle; resembling a panicle.

Pannose. With the texture of felt or closely woven woolen cloth.

Papery. Thin and usually whitish like paper. Compare chartaceous which is usually thick-papery.

Papilionaceous. Like the "sweetpea" type flower of Leguminosae with standard (banner) wings and keel. Fig. 414.

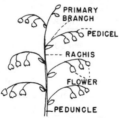

PANDURATE LEAF
Fig. 412.

PANICLE
Fig. 413.

PAPILIONACEOUS FLOWER
Fig. 414.

Papilla (pl. papillae). A minute nipple-shaped projection. Fig. 415.

PAPILLAE
Fig. 415.

Papillose. Bearing papillae.

Pappus. The modified calyx limb in Compositae, forming a crown of various character at the summit of the achene. Fig. 416.

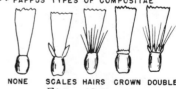

PAPPUS TYPES OF COMPOSITAE

NONE   SCALES   HAIRS   CROWN   DOUBLE
Fig. 416.

172

Parallel veined. A leaf with the
veins running parallel to each
other, usually all about the
same size (except sometimes
the midrib) and the connections
between obscure. Characteristic
of the leaf of Monocotyledon-
eae. Fig. 417.

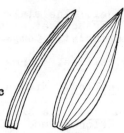

PARALLEL VEINED LEAVES
Fig. 417.

Parasite. An organism growing upon and obtaining
nourishment from another; usually lacking
chlorophyll in plants.

Parasitic. Like a parasite.

Parietal. Borne on or pertaining to the wall or
inner surface of an ovary
or fruit. Drawing number
1 shows only one placenta,
number 2 has two placentae
showing. Fig. 418.

(2.)   (1.)
PARIETAL PLACENTATION
Fig. 418.

Parted. Lobed or cut in over
half-way and usually very
near to the base or midrib.
The sinuses and segments
may be sharp or rounded.
Fig. 419.

PINNATELY   PALMATELY
PARTED LEAVES
Fig. 419.

Pectinate. Pinnatifid with the segments narrow and arranged like the
teeth of a comb; comb-like.
Fig. 420.

PECTINATE LEAF
Fig. 420.

173

Pedicel. The stalk to a single flower of an inflorescence; also used as a stalk to a grass
spikelet. Compare peduncle.

Pedicellate. Borne on a pedicel.

Pedicelled. With a pedicel. Same as pedicellate.

Peduncle. The stalk to a solitary flower or to an
inflorescence. Compare pedicel. Fig. 421.

Pedunculate. Borne upon a peduncle.

Pellucid. Clear and transparent.

Peltate. Shield-shaped, attached to the center or
near the center, at least in-a-ways from the
margin, on the order of an umbrella. Fig. 422.

Pendulous. More or less hanging or declined.

Penta-. Used as a prefix meaning "five".

Pepo. The fleshy indehiscent fruit characteristic
of the Cucurbitaceae. It differs from a berry
chiefly by having a hard, more or less thickened
rind.

Perennial. A plant lasting for 3 or more years; a
stem not dying back over winter.

Perfect. A flower with both functional stamens and
pistils.

Perfoliate. Where the leaf has the stem apparently
passing through it, or where opposite leaves are
joined around the stem at their bases. Fig. 423.

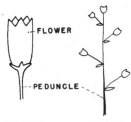

SOLITARY   RACEME
FLOWER   PELTATE LEAF   PERFOLIATE STEMS
Fig. 421.   Fig. 422.   Fig. 423.

174

Perianth. The floral envelope consisting of calyx
and corolla however incomplete or modified.
Used particularly when the calyx and corolla cannot be readily distinguished.

Pericarp. The wall of the ripened ovary and therefore the wall of the fruit. Sometimes 3 layers
can be distinguished, the exocarp (outer),
mesocarp (middle) and endocarp (inner). See
drupe.

Perigynous. Situated around but
not attached to the ovary or
its base directly; a flower with
stamens and pistils on the calyx
tube and the ovary superior.
Fig. 424.

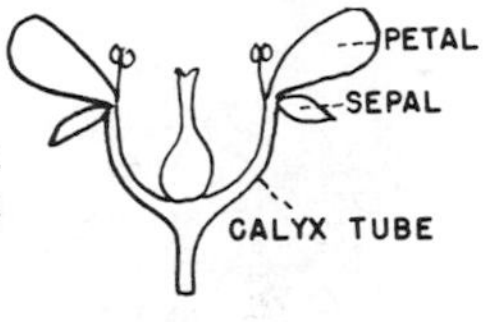

PERIGYNOUS FLOWER
Fig. 424.

Persistent. Remaining attached after like parts
ordinarily fall off.

Personate. Two-lipped (as a corolla) the throat
closed by a prominent palate. See palate for
drawing.

Petal. One of the individual parts of the corolla,
used particularly for a polypetalous corolla in
designating one unit.

Petaloid. Resembling a petal
in some way, usually colored other than green.

Petiolate. With a petiole.

Petiole. The stalk to a leaf
blade or to a compound
leaf. Fig. 425.

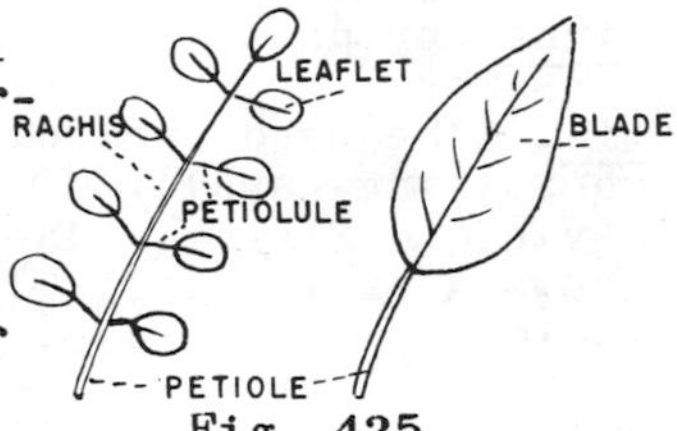

Fig. 425.

Petiolule. The stalk to a leaflet in a compound
leaf. For drawing see petiole.

Phyllary. A special name sometimes
used for an involucral bract on
the head of Compositae.

Pilose. With long soft straight
hairs. Fig. 426.

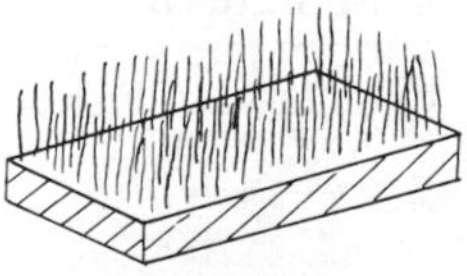

PILOSE
Fig. 426.

175

Pinna (pl. pinnae). One of the first or primary divisions of a pinnately compound or decompound
leaf; used especially in ferns. Fig. 427.

Pinnate. Compound leaf with the leaflets on 2 opposite sides of an elongated axis. Fig. 428.

Pinnatifid. Pinnately lobed, cleft or parted
usually $\frac{1}{2}$ way in to the midrib or more. Fig.
429.

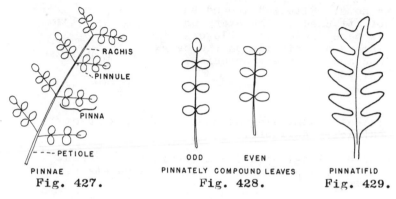

PINNAE   PINNATELY COMPOUND LEAVES   PINNATIFID
Fig. 427.   Fig. 428.   Fig. 429.

Pinnule. The pinnate segment of a
pinna in a bipinnate leaf. In a
tripinnate leaf the pinnules are
again pinnately divided. See
pinna for drawing.

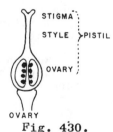

Pistil. The seed-producing organ,
consisting usually of ovary,
style and stigma. The drawing
shows a pistil split longitudinally. Fig. 430.

Fig. 430.

Pistillate. Provided with pistils,
used when stamens are lacking.

Pith. The spongy center of a stem,
surrounding or joining to the
inner part of the vascular
bundles. Fig. 431

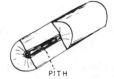

Fig. 431.

176

Pitted. Marked with small depressions
    or pits. Fig. 432.

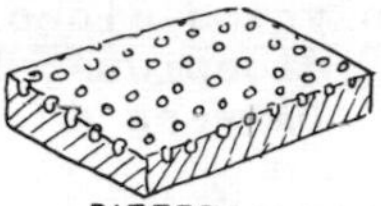

PITTED

Fig. 432.

Placenta (pl. placentae). Any part of the interior
    of an ovary that bears ovules. See parietal,
    axile and free central placentation.

Plane. With flat surface.

Plano-convex. An object usually a
    fruit or seed, flat on one side and
    convex on the other. The drawing
    shows a seed cut in 2 sections.
    Fig. 433.

PLANO
CONVEX SEED

Fig. 433.

Plicate. Folded in plaits, usually lengthwise on
    the order of a folding fan. Fig. 434.

Plumose. Hairs with side hairs along the main axis
    like the plume of a feather. Fig. 435.

Plumule. The stem- and leaf-producing structure of
    an embryo in the seed.

Pod. Any dry dehiscent fruit, often used as a
    synonym for legume.

Pollen. The male spores in an anther.

Pollinium (pl. pollinia). A mass of waxy or coher-
    ent pollen grains as in Asclepias or Orchidaceae.
    Fig. 436.

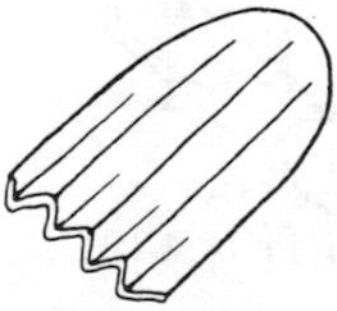

PLICATE
Fig. 434.

PLUMOSE STYLE
Fig. 435.

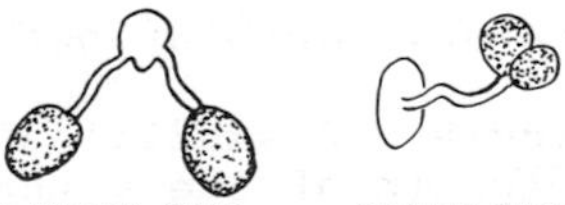

MILKWEED TYPE   ORCHID TYPE
POLLINIA
Fig. 436.

177

Polygamo-dioecious. Polygamous but chiefly
dioecious; having bisexual flowers and unisexual
flowers on separate individuals.

Polygamo-monoecious. Polygamous but chiefly monoecious; having bisexual flowers and unisexual
flowers on the same individual.

Polygamous. Having bisexual flowers and unisexual
flowers on the same or on different individuals.
This term is not always uniformly used.

Polymorphous. With several forms;
variable as to habit.

Polypetalous. The petals completely separate from each other.

Polysepalous. Calyx with separate
sepals.

POME
LONG SECTION
Fig. 437.

Pome. A fleshy indehiscent fruit with
an inferior ovary and more than one
locule; of the apple type.
Fig. 437.

PORES

Poricidal fruit. A dehiscent fruit,
the seeds escaping through pores.
Fig. 438.

PORICIDAL CAPSULE
Fig. 438.

Posterior. On the side next to or
close to the axis. Compare anterior.

Precocious. Appearing or developing
very early; used in Salix where the
aments develop before the leaves.

Prickle. A small, usually slender outgrowth of the young bark, coming
off with it. Compare spine and
thorn. Fig. 439.

PRICKLES
Fig. 439.

Primocane. The first year's cane (shoot), usually
flowerless in the brambles (Rubus).

178

Procumbent. Lying or trailing on the ground, usually not rooting at the nodes. See prostrate. Fig. 440.

PROCUMBENT STEM

Fig. 440.

Proliferous. Producing bulbs or plantlets from leaves or other offshoots.

Prostrate. Lying flat on the ground, if a stem then may or may not root at nodes. See procumbent for drawing.

Prothallus (pl. prothallia). A usually flat thallus-like growth resulting from the germination of a spore, upon which are produced sexual organs or new plants.

Proximad. Toward the point of attachment.

Proximal. The end of an organ by which it is attached.

Pruinose. With a waxy powdery usually whitish covering, this usually rubbing off readily; glaucous to a conspicuous degree.

Pseudo-. A prefix meaning false.

Puberulent. With very short hairs; minutely pubescent. Fig. 441.

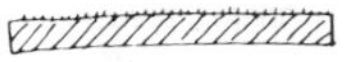

PUBERULENT
Fig. 441.

Pubescent. Loosely used for covered with hairs; technically with short soft hairs. Fig. 442.

PUBESCENT

Fig. 442.

Pulvinate. Cushioned or shaped like a close thick mat or cushion.

Punctate. Dotted with depressions, or with transluscent internal glands or colored dots.

Puncticulate. Minutely punctate.

PUNGENT LEAF TEETH
Fig. 443.

Pungent. Tipped with a sharp rigid point. Fig. 443.

179

Pustulose. Beset with pimple-
like elevated areas. Same
as pustulate. Fig. 444.

PUSTULOSE
Fig. 444.

Pyriform. Pear-shaped. Fig. 445.

Pyxis. A capsule with circumscissle dehiscence, the
top coming off as a lid. Fig. 446.

Quill-like. Terete, more or less tapering, usually
hollow. Fig. 447.

PYRIFORM FRUIT
Fig. 445.

PYXIS
Fig. 446.

QUILL-LIKE LEAF
Fig. 447.

Quinate. With five nearly similar
structures (as leaflets) from a common point. Fig. 448.

QUINATE LEAFLETS
Fig. 448.

Raceme. An inflorescence with pedicelled
flowers borne along a more or less
elongated axis with the younger flowers
nearest the apex. Fig. 449.

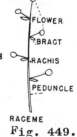

FLOWER
BRACT
RACHIS
PEDUNCLE

RACEME
Fig. 449.

Racemiform. In the form of a raceme.

Racemose. Raceme-like or bearing racemes.

Rachilla. A small rachis; applied particularly to the axis of a grass spikelet, and to the secondary axis in sedges.

Rachis. The central elongated axis to an inflorescence or a compound leaf. See raceme for example.

Radiate. Spreading from or arranged around a common center. In Compositae meaning with ray-flowers.

Radical. Belonging to the root, or apparently arising from or very near the root. The leaves of dandelion are called radical. Compare rosette. Fig. 450.

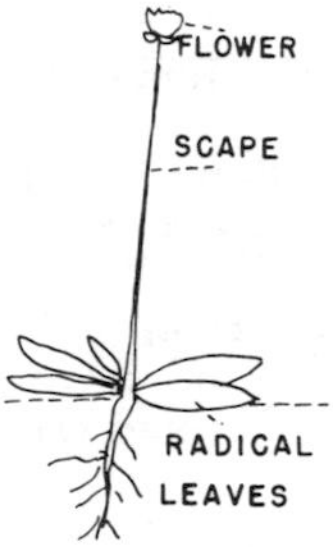

FLOWER

SCAPE

RADICAL LEAVES

Fig. 450.

Rank. A vertical row; for example leaves that are 2-ranked are in 2 rows along the stem.

Ray. The branch of an umbel or a similar inflorescence. The ligulate or strap-shaped flower in the Compositae, used especially for marginal flowers different from the central regular ones. Fig. 451.

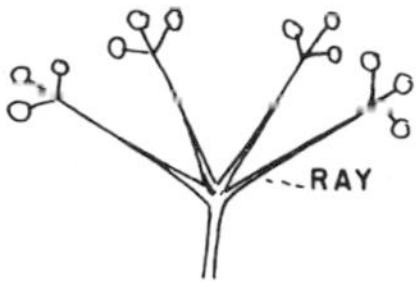

RAY

UMBELLIFERAE
Fig. 451 1st

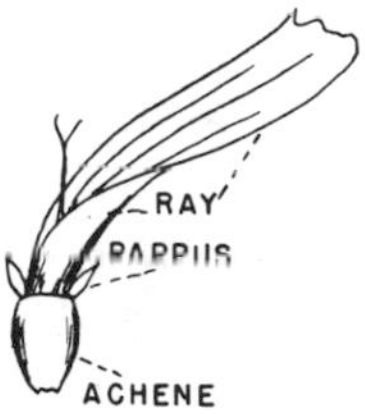

RAY
PAPPUS
ACHENE

COMPOSITAE
Fig. 451 2nd

Receptacle. The more or less expanded portion of the flower stalk that bears the organs of a flower or the collected flowers of a head as in Compositae.

Reclinate. Turned or bent abruptly downward.

Reclining. Lying upon something.

Recumbent. Leaning or reposing upon the ground.

Recurved. Curved outward, downward or backward.

181

Reflexed. Abruptly bent or turned downward or backward.

Regular. A flower with all the members of each set
alike in form, size and color; radially symmetrical.

Reniform. Kidney-shaped, usually attached at the
center of the incurved side. Fig. 452.

Repand. With a wavy surface or margin, not as deep
as sinuate. Same as undulate.

Replum. The septum of certain dry dehiscent fruits,
persisting after the valves have fallen away;
used in the Cruciferae. Fig. 453.

Reticulate. In the form of a network; leaf veins in
a network. Fig. 454.

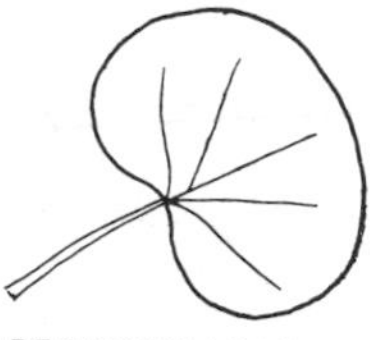

RENIFORM LEAF
Fig. 452.

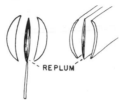

REPLUM

Fig. 453.

RETICULATE SURFACE
Fig. 454.

Retrorse. Directed backward or downward.

Retuse. A rounded apex with a shallow
notch. Fig. 455.

RETUSE APEX
Fig. 455.

Revolute. Rolled backward from each
margin upon the lower side. Opposite of involute. Fig. 456.

REVOLUTE LEAF
Fig. 456.

Rhizoid. Root-like but of simple structure.

Rhizomatous. Having the characters of a rhizome.
Sometimes written rhizomatose.

Rhizome. Any prostrate more or
less elongated stem growing
partly or completely beneath
the surface of the ground; usually rooting at the nodes and
becoming upcurved at apex.
See rootstock. Fig. 457.

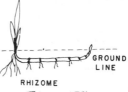

GROUND LINE

RHIZOME

Fig. 457.

Rhombic. Outline of an equilateral
oblique-angled figure; 4-sided
like a diamond shape. Fig. 458.

RHOMBIC LEAF
Fig. 458.

Rhomboid. A solid figure rhombic in outline.

Rib. A primary or prominent vein usually of a leaf.

Root. The descending axis of the plant, without
nodes and internodes and absorbing moisture from
the ground. Roots may appear, however, in unusual places (see adventitious).

Rootlet. A small root; often used for the aerial
supporting roots put out by some vines.

Rootstock. A root-like stem or branch
under or sometimes on the ground.
Like rhizome but loosely used by
some to include any elongated underground structure that spreads the
plant.

SCAPE

Rosette. A dense basal cluster of
leaves arranged in circular fashion
like the leaves of the common dandelion. Fig. 459.

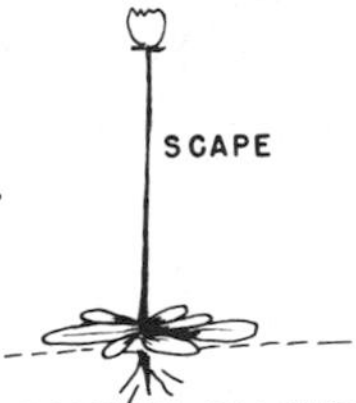

ROSETTE OF LEAVES
Fig. 459.

Rostrate. Having a beak.
Fig. 460.

BEAKED FRUIT   BEAK OF KEEL
(OXYTROPIS)

ROSTRATE
Fig. 460.

183

Rosulate. In the form of a rosette.

Rotate. A wheel-shaped corolla with short tube and wide horizontally flaring limb. Fig. 461.

Rudiment. An imperfectly developed, usually minute organ.

Rufous. Reddish-brown.

Rugose. With wrinkled or creased surface. Fig. 462.

Rugulose. Minutely rugose.

Runcinate. Sharply incised or pinnatifid with the segments directed backward. Fig. 463.

ROTATE COROLLA
Fig. 461.

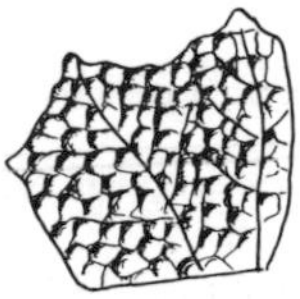

RUGOSE SURFACE
Fig. 462.

RUNCINATE LEAF
Fig. 463.

Runner. A very slender or filiform stolon-like stem rooting at the apex. Fig. 464.

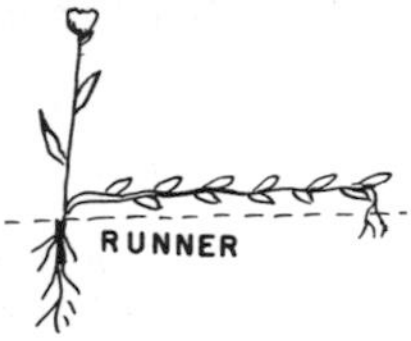

RUNNER

Fig. 464.

Rush-like. Grass-like in general appearance, the flowers usually not colored or conspicuous.

Saccate. Sac-shaped or pouch-shaped.

Sagittate. Shaped like an arrow-head with the basal lobes directed backward. Compare hastate. Fig. 465.

SAGITTATE LEAF
Fig. 465.

Salverform. A corolla with a long slender tube, abruptly flaring into a circular limb. Fig. 466.

Samara. A dry indehiscent winged fruit. Fig. 467.

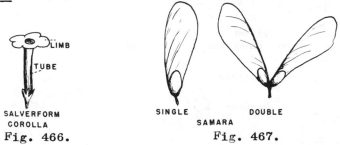

SALVERFORM
COROLLA
Fig. 466.

SINGLE   DOUBLE
SAMARA
Fig. 467.

Saprophyte. A plant that lives on dead organic material, usually lacking green chlorophyll. Compare parasite.

Scaberulent. Slightly scabrous.

Scaberulous. Slightly scabrous.

Scabrous. Rough or harsh to the touch usually from very short stiff hairs or short sharp projections. The test is to draw the finger tip lightly over the surface. The drawing shows a surface scabrous from short sharp projections. Fig. 468.

SCABROUS
Fig. 468.

Scale. Any thin scarious body resembling the scale of a fish or reptile; often used for such structures present on the basal or underground portion of the plant. Compare bract.

Scape. A naked flowering stem rising from the ground without proper leaves. For a drawing see "radical".

Scapose. Bearing a scape or resembling one.

Scarious. Thin, dry, membranous and more or less transluscent, not green.

Schizocarp. A dry fruit of 2 or more carpels,
splitting up at maturity into 2 or more one-
seeded, indehiscent segments. Some manuals call
this fruit a cremocarp at least in part.
Fig. 469.

Scorpioid. Coiled at the apex like the tail of a
scorpion, used especially for inflorescences.
Fig. 470.

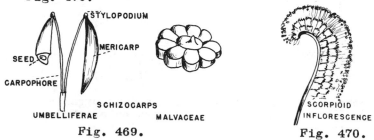

STYLOPODIUM

MERICARP

SEED

CARPOPHORE

SCHIZOCARPS

UMBELLIFERAE   MALVACEAE

Fig. 469.

SCORPIOID
INFLORESCENCE

Fig. 470.

Scurfy. Covered with small scale-like or bran-like
particles.

Secund. Borne or directed to 1 side of the axis.
Fig. 471.

Seed. The matured ovule, consisting of embryo and
its coats, with a supply of food.

Sepal. One of the parts of the outer whorl of the
floral envelope or calyx, usually green in color.

Sepaloid. Of the color or texture of a sepal, or
resembling one in some way.

Septate. Divided by one or more partitions. Illustrated for a twig but can be in other
structures. Fig. 472.

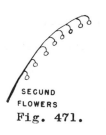

SECUND
FLOWERS

Fig. 471.

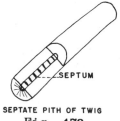

SEPTUM

SEPTATE PITH OF TWIG

Fig. 472.

186

Septicidal. A capsule splitting down
the septa and not through the
locule. Compare loculicidal.
Fig. 473.

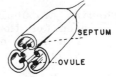

SEPTICIDAL CAPSULE
Fig. 473.

Septum. Any kind of a partition.

Sericeous. Covered with long, straight, soft, appressed hairs giving a silky texture. The hairs
are usually more numerous than in the drawing.
Fig. 474.

Serrate. With sharp teeth directed forward. Fig.
475.

SERICEOUS
Fig. 474.

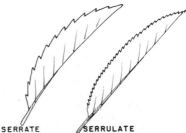

SERRATE   SERRULATE
Fig. 475.

Serrulate. Serrate with small teeth. See serrate
for drawing.

Sessile. Without a stalk of
any kind. Fig. 476.

Seta (pl. setae). A bristle-
like hair.

Setaceous. Bristle-like.

Setiform. Like or on the order of
a bristle.

Setose. Beset with bristles.
Fig. 477.

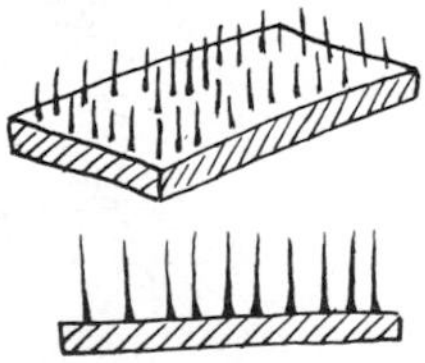

SESSILE
Fig. 476.

SETOSE SURFACE
Fig. 477.

Sheath. A tubular envelope, usually
　　used for that part of the leaf
　　of a sedge or grass that en-
　　velopes the stem.

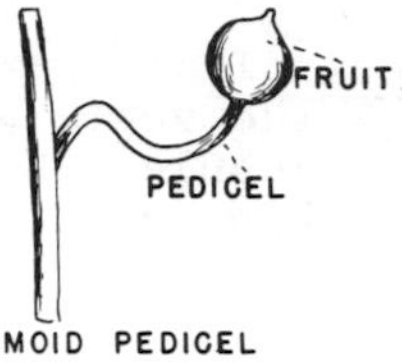

SIGMOID PEDICEL
Fig. 478.

Shrub. A woody perennial plant smal-
　　ler than a tree and usually with
　　several basal stems. Compare
　　tree with its drawings.

Sigmoid. Doubly-curved like the letter S. Fig.
　　478.

Silicle. A short fruit of the
　　family Cruciferae (mustards)
　　usually not more than twice
　　as long as wide. Fig. 479.

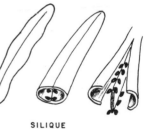

SILICLE

Fig. 479.

Silique. A fruit of the
　　mustard family (Cruciferae),
　　dry, dehiscent and 2-celled,
　　the septum (replum) thin
　　with the 2 halves of the
　　fruit pulling away from it.
　　Often used to designate a
　　mustard fruit that is
　　elongated and longer than
　　a silicle. Fig. 480.

SILIQUE
Fig. 480.

Silky. Of silk-like appearance caused by long,
　　straight, soft, appressed hairs. See sericeous.

Simple. Of only 1 part, not completely
　　divided into separate segments.
　　Compare compound. Fig. 481.

SIMPLE LEAF
Fig. 481.

Sinuate. Strongly wavy-margined,
deeper than undulate or repand.
Fig. 482.

SINUATE MARGIN
Fig. 482.

Sinus. The depression or recess between 2 adjoining
lobes. Fig. 483.

Smooth. Surface not rough, sometimes loosely used
for absence of any hair.

Sordid. Dirty in tint.

Sorus (pl. sori). A cluster of sporangia on a fern
frond. The figures show types of indusia.
Fig. 484.

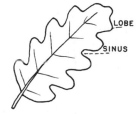

LOBE

SINUS

SINUS
Fig. 483.

MARGIN OF FROND

PELTATE

LATERAL

INFERIOR

SORI OF FERN
Fig. 484.

Spadix. A spike with a thick and fleshy axis, usually densely flowered with imperfect flowers.
In the figure the lower part of the spathe is
cut away to show the lower flowers of the
spadix. Fig. 485.

Spathe. A large bract sheathing or enclosing an
inflorescence.

Spatulate. Broad
and rounded at
apex and taper-
ing at base, like
a druggist's spat-
ula; flattened
spoon-shaped.
Fig. 486.

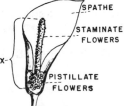

SPATHE

STAMINATE
FLOWERS

SPADIX-

PISTILLATE
FLOWERS

Fig. 485.

SPATULATE LEAF
Fig. 486.

189

Spherical. A 3-dimensional solid, round in outline, like the earth. Same as globose.

Spicate. Arranged in or resembling a spike.

Spike. An inflorescence with the flowers sessile on a more or less elongated axis with the younger flowers at the apex. Fig. 487.

FLOWER
RACHIS
SPIKE

Fig. 487

Spike-like. Resembling a spike, used where the flowers are on short pedicels or on very short panicle branches.

Spindle-shaped. Broadest at about the middle and tapering both ways. See fusiform for drawing.

Spine. A sharp-pointed rigid deep-seated outgrowth from the stem, not pulling off with the bark. Compare prickle. Sometimes differentiated from thorn by absence of vascular tissue. Fig. 488.

SPINE

Fig. 488.

Spinescent. Bearing a spine or ending in a spine-like sharp point.

Spinulose. Minutely spiny; beset with small spines.

ANNULUS

Sporangium (pl. sporangia). The spore-bearing case in Pteridophytes. Fig. 489.

SPORANGIUM
FERN

Fig. 489.

Spore. The small reproductive body in Pteridophytes.

Sporocarp. The fruit-cases of certain Pteridophytes containing sporangia or spores.

Sporophyll. A spore-bearing leaf, often highly modified.

Sporophyte. The spore-bearing, asexual generation. Used especially in Pteridophytes for the conspicuous plant body. Compare gametophyte.

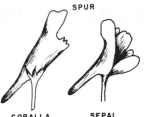

SPUR

CORALLA   SEPAL
SPURRED   SPURRED
Fig. 490.

Sprawling. Lying on or leaning upon or over another object.

Spreading. Diverging nearly at right angles; nearly prostrate.

Spur. A hollow, sac-like or tubular extension of a floral organ, usually nectariferous. Fig. 490.

Squamella (pl. squamellae). A small chaffy bract or scale-like appendage.

Squarrose. Having the parts or processes (usually the tips) spreading or recurved. The drawing shows squarrose bracts of a composite head, the flowers shed. Fig. 491.

SQUARROSE
BRACTS
Fig. 491.

Stamen. One of the pollen-bearing organs of a flower. Made up of filament and anther. Fig. 492.

Staminal tube. The united part of the filaments when this occurs. Fig. 493.

Staminate. Bearing stamens only.

Staminodium (pl. staminodia). A sterile stamen or any structure lacking an anther but corresponding to a stamen. Also written "staminode". Fig. 494.

ANTHER

FILAMENT

STAMEN
Fig. 192.

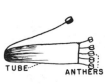

TUBE
ANTHERS

STAMINAL TUBE
Fig. 493.

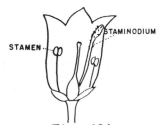

STAMINODIUM

STAMEN

Fig. 494.

191

Standard. Same as banner.

Stellate. Star-like or star-shaped with slender segments or hairs radiating out from a common center. Fig. 495.

STELLATE HAIRS
Fig. 495.

Sterile. Infertile and unproductive, as a flower without a pistil, a stamen without an anther or a leafy shoot without flowers.

Stigma. That part of the pistil that receives the pollen, usually at or near the apex of the pistil and mostly hairy, papillose or sticky. See ovary for drawing.

Stigmatic. Belonging to or having the characteristics of a stigma.

Stipe. The stalk-like support of a pistil (above the other flower parts). Also the name for the petiole of a fern frond. Fig. 496.

Fig. 496. Fig. 496.
1st   2nd

Stipel. An appendage like a stipule but subtending the leaflet. See stipule for drawing.

Stipitate. Provided with a stipe or with a slender stalk-like base.

Stipulate. Provided with stipules.

Stipule. An appendage at the base of the petiole or leaf at each side of its insertion; often more or less united. Fig. 497.

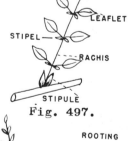

Fig. 497.

Stolon. A trailing shoot above ground rooting at the nodes. Compare runner. Fig. 498.

Fig. 498.

192

Stoloniferous. Bearing stolons.

Stoloniform. On the general order of a stolon.

Stomate (pl. stomata). A small opening on the surface of a leaf through which gaseous exchange
takes place. Sometimes written stoma.

STRICT

Stramineous. Straw-colored.

Striate. Marked with fine longitudinal
lines, grooves, furrows or streaks.

Strict. Very straight and upright.
Fig. 499.

Fig. 499.

Strigillose. Like strigose but
hairs very short.

Strigose. With appressed, stiff,
rather short hairs. Fig. 500.

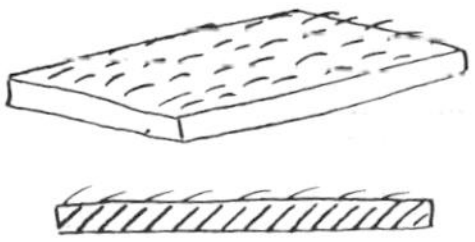

STRIGOSE

Fig. 500.

Strobilus (pl. strobili). An inflorescence char-
acterized by imbricated bracts or scales as a
pine cone. See cone for drawing.

Strophiole. An appendage at the hilum of some seeds.

Style. The usually stalk-like part of a pistil connecting the ovary and stigma. See ovary for
drawing.

Stylopodium. A disk-like expansion of the base of
the style as in Umbelliferae. See schizocarp
for drawing.

Sub-. A prefix meaning almost or below.

Subtending. Situated closely beneath something,
often enclosing or embracing it.

Subulate. Awl-shaped; narrowly triangular and tapering to a sharp point. Fig. 501.

SUBULATE LEAF
Fig. 501.

Succulent. Fleshy and full of juice.

Suffruticose. Low-shrubby; applied to perennials, the lower part of the stems woody but the upper part herbaceous. Also written **suffrutescent.**

Sulcate. Grooved or furrowed, especially if the groove is deep and longitudinal. Fig. 502.

SULCATE STEM
Fig. 502.

Sulcus. (pl. **sulci**). A furrow or groove.

Superior ovary. An ovary with the perianth inserted below it. Fig. 503.

SUPERIOR OVARY
Fig. 503.

Surculose-proliferous. Producing runners or offsets from the base or from rootstocks.

Suture. A junction or seam of union; a line of dehiscence. Fig. 504.

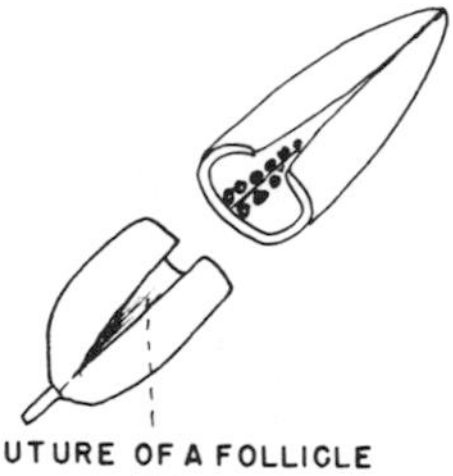

SUTURE OF A FOLLICLE
Fig. 504.

Sympetalous. Petals more or less united. Same as **gamopetalous.**

Synsepalous. The sepals more or less united. Same as **gamosepalous.**

Taproot. The primary root continuing the axis of the plant downward. Such roots may be thick as in the drawing or comparatively thin. Fig. 505.

TAP ROOT

Fig. 505.

194

Tawny. Dull yellowish with a tinge of brown.

Taxon (pl. taxa). A general term for any morpho-
     logical unit or group.

Tendril. A slender
     cauline or fol-
     iar outgrowth.
     Commonly coil-
     ing at apex and
     serving as an
     organ of sup-
     port. Fig. 506.

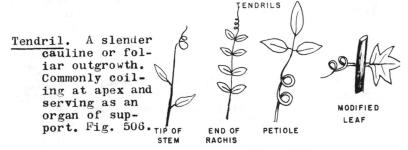

Fig. 506.

Terete. Circular in cross-section and
     more or less elongated. Like cylind-
     rical but may be slightly tapering.
     Fig. 507.

TERETE STEM
Fig. 507.

Tornate. Arranged in three's.

Terrestrial. A plant growing in the air with its
     basal parts in soil. Compare aquatic with parts
     immersed in water.

Tessellate. Checkered.

Tetra-angular. With 4 angles.

Thalloid. Resembling or on the order of a thallus.

Thallus. A vegetative often flattened body not dif-
     ferentiated into stems and leaves.

Thorn. A stiff, hard, sharp-pointed
     emergence more deeply seated than a
     prickle. By some, differentiated
     from a spine in having vascular tis-
     sue. Fig. 508.

THORN

Fig. 508.

Throat. The orifice of a gemopetalous
corolla or calyx, at or just below
the junction of the tube with the
limb. Fig. 509.

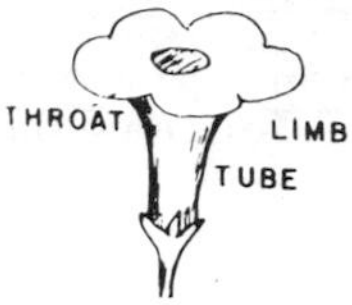

Fig. 509.

Thyrse. A contracted, cylindrical or ovoid-
pyramidal, usually densely flowered
panicle, like a cluster of grapes. Also written thrysus. Fig. 510.

THYRSE
Fig. 510.

Thyrsoid. Resembling a thyrse.

Tomentose. With a dense wool-like covering of matted, intertangled hairs of
medium length. Compare lanate and
canescent. Fig. 511.

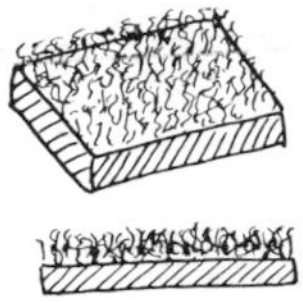

TOMENTOSE
Fig. 511.

Tomentulose. Sparingly or minutely tomentose.

Tomentum. The covering of closely interwoven and tangled hairs in a tomentose surface.

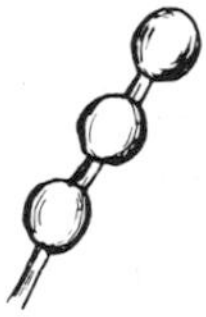

Torose. Cylindrical in shape with swell-
ings and contractions at intervals.
Fig. 512.

TOROSE FRUIT
Fig. 512.

Tortuous. Twisted or bent.

Torulose. Minutely torose as in a small pod constricted between seeds.

Torus. Same as receptacle.

Trailing. Prostrate but not rooting.

Translucent. Transmitting rays of light without being transparent.

Tree. A perennial woody plant of considerable
stature at maturity and with 1 or few main
trunks. Rather loosely used but a fairly well
understood concept. Fig. 513.

Trichome. A hair-like outgrowth of the epidermis.

Trifoliate. A compound leaf with 3 leaflets.
Fig. 514.

TREE   SHRUB
Fig. 513.

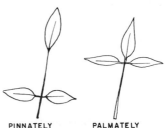

PINNATELY   PALMATELY
TRIFOLIATE
Fig. 514.

Trigonal. Three-angled. Fig. 515.

TRIGONAL STEM
Fig. 515.

Trigonous. Three-angled. Same
as trigonal.

Tripinnate. Pinnately compound
3 times; the pinnules again
pinnate. Fig. 516.

TRIPINNATE LEAF
Fig. 516.

Triquetrous. With 3 salient angles,
the sides concave or chanelled.
Fig. 517.

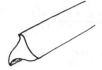

TRIQUETROUS
Fig. 517.

Triternate. Three times ternate;
ternate with the 3 main divisions
once and once-again ternate.
Fig. 518.

TRITERNATE LEAF
Fig. 518.

Truncate. Squared at the tip or
base as if cut off with a
straight blade. Fig. 519.

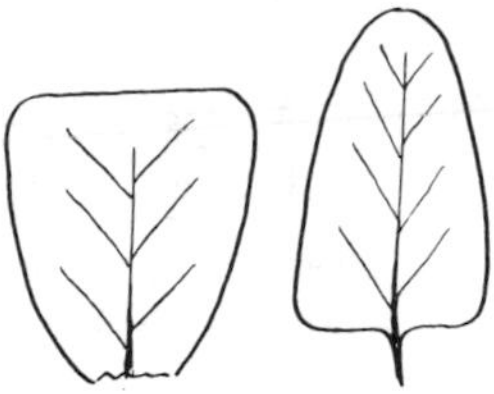

APEX   BASE
TRUNCATE LEAF
Fig. 519.

Tube. Any hollow cylindrical structure, especially
the tubular basal part of a gamopetalous corolla.

Tuber. A thickened, short usually
subterranean stem having numerous
buds called eyes; like a potato.
Fig. 520.

TUBER
Fig. 520.

Tubercle. A small rounded structure,
often pimple-like. Fig. 521.

TUBERCLES
Fig. 521.

Tuberculate. Bearing small processes or tubercles.

Tufted. Having a cluster of hairs or other slender outgrowths; stems in a very close cluster.

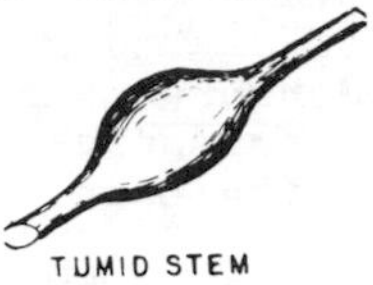

Tumid. Swollen. Fig. 522.

TUMID STEM
Fig. 522.

Tunicated. Having concentric coats as an onion bulb. See bulb for drawing.

Turbinate. Top-shaped; inversely conical. About the same as obconical which see for drawing.

Turgid. Swollen or tightly drawn; said of a thin covering expanded by internal pressure.

Turion. A scaly often succulent shoot produced from a bud on an underground rootstock.

Twining. Ascending by coiling around a support.

Type. In taxonomy the specimens from which the original description was made. (Type specimens.)

Umbel. A convex or flat-topped inflorescence, the flowers all arising from 1 point, the younger in the center. Fig. 523.

Umbellate. In or like an umbel.

Umbellet. A small or secondary umbel in a compound umbel. See umbel for drawing.

Umbonate. Bearing a stout projection in the center; bossed. Fig. 524.

Uncinate. Hooked near the apex or in the form of a hook. Fig. 525.

SIMPLE   COMPOUND
UMBEL
Fig. 523.

UMBONATE
Fig. 524.

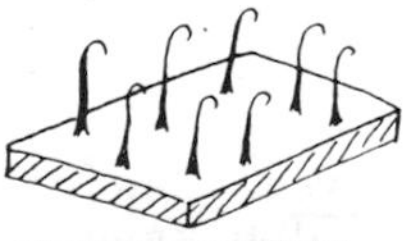

UNCINATE BRISTLES
Fig. 525.

Undershrub. A small shrub or a
   perennial plant woody only at
   the base.

Undulate. The margin gently wavy.
   Same as repand. Compare
   sinuate. Fig. 526.

UNDULATE MARGIN
Fig. 526.

Unifoliate. A theoretically compound leaf with all
   but 1 leaflet suppressed; a simple-appearing
   leaf in a group with compound leaves.

Unilateral. Arranged on one side.

Uniseriate. Arranged in one row or series.

Unisexual. With either stamens or pistils, not both.
   Compare bisexual and perfect.

Urceolate. Hollow and cylindrical or ovoid
   but contracted at or near the mouth
   like an urn. Fig. 527.

Urn-shaped. Same as urceolate.

URCEOLATE
COROLLA
Fig. 527.

Utricle. A small thin-walled 1-seeded fruit; any
   bladder-like body.

Vaginate. Provided with or surrounded by a sheath.

Valvate. Opening by valves or
   provided with valves; also
   for parts meeting together
   edge to edge without overlapping. Compare imbricate.
   Fig. 528.

VALVATE SEPALS IN BUD
X SECT.
Fig. 528.

Valve. One of the parts or segments into which a
   dehiscent fruit splits.

200

Vascular bundle. An elongated group of cells specialized for conduction and often support. In a leaf, the veins.

Vein. Threads of vascular tissue in a leaf or other organ especially those which branch. Compare nerve.

Velum. The fold on the inner side of the leaf base of Isoetes functioning as an indusium.

Ventral. Belonging to the inner or axis side of an organ; the upper surface of a leaf.

Ventricose. Inflated or swollen unequally as on one side. In the drawing the corolla tube is ventricose at its base. Fig. 529.

VENTRICOSE
COROLLA
Fig. 529.

Vernation. The particular arrangement of a leaf or its parts in the bud.

Verrucose. Covered with wart-like elevations. Fig. 530.

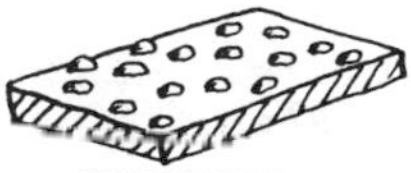

VERRUCOSE
Fig. 530.

Versatile. An anther attached at or near its middle and turning freely on its support. Compare basifixed. Fig. 531.

VERSATILE
ANTHER
Fig. 531

Verticil. A circle of 3 or more structures around a common axis.

Verticillate. With 3 or more
leaves or other structures
arranged in a circle about a
stem or other common axis.
Same as whorled. In the
drawing the leaves are very
narrow. Fig. 532.

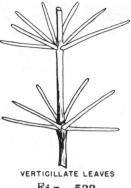

VERTICILLATE LEAVES
Fig. 532.

Villous. With long, soft, somewhat
wavy hairs. Compare pilose.
Fig. 533.

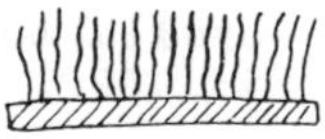

VILLOUS
Fig. 533.

Vine. A plant climbing or scrambling on some support, the stem not standing upright of itself.

Virgate. Wand-like, as a slender straight erect
stem.

Viscid. Glutinous, sticky or gummy to the touch.

Weed. A troublesome or aggressive plant that in-
trudes where not wanted. especially a plant that
vigorously colonizes disturbed areas. To the
rangeman a weed is a herbaceous nongrass-like
plant on the range.

Whorled. With 3 or more leaves or other structures
arranged in a circle around a stem or some common axis. Same as verticillate which see for
sketch.

Wing. Any membranous or thin expansion bordering or
surrounding an organ. Also one of the lateral
petals in a papilionaceous corolla. See banner
for sketch.

Winged. Provided with wings.

Winter annual. A plant where the seed germinates in the fall, the seedling surviving the winter and completing its growth in the spring of the next season.

Woolly. With long, soft interwoven hair. Same as lanate which see for drawing.

Xerophyte. A plant adapted to dry or arid habitats. Compare mesophyte and hydrophyte.

Zygomorphic. With inequality in the size, form or union of its similar parts; not radially symmetrical. See irregular flower for sketches.